Fodor's
25 Best

TORONTO

How to Use This Book

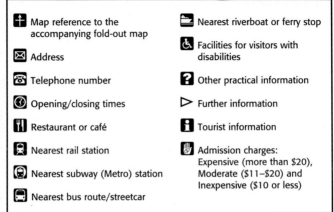

This guide is divided into four sections

● Essential Toronto: An introduction to the city and tips on making the most of your stay.

● Toronto by Area: We've broken the city into five areas, and recommended the best sights, shops, entertainment venues, nightlife and places to eat in each one. Suggested walks help you to explore on foot.

● Where to Stay: The best hotels, whether you're looking for luxury, budget or something in between.

● Need to Know: The info you need to make your trip run smoothly, including getting about by public transport, weather tips, emergency phone numbers and useful websites.

Navigation In the Toronto by Area chapter, we've given each area its own color, which is also used on the locator maps throughout the book and the map on the inside front cover.

Maps The fold-out map with this book is a comprehensive street plan of Toronto. The grid on this fold-out map is the same as the grid on the locator maps within the book. We've given grid references within the book for each sight and listing.

Contents

Introducing Toronto

Canada's foremost tourism destination, Toronto is vibrant, vivacious and good-looking, with stunning modern architecture alongside the lively lakeshore, and world-class entertainment and shopping alongside characterful multicultural neighborhoods.

Ottawa may be the capital, but Toronto is where it's at, and neither the soaring cost of real estate nor the summer smog that occasionally covers downtown has stopped it becoming North America's fourth-largest city and Canada's top tourist destination.

Immigrants still arrive at the rate of around 100,000 a year, and their diversity has made Toronto one of the most multicultural cities in the world. This is no melting pot, though; it's a honeycomb of colorful neighborhoods offering a world of atmospheres, from exotic Asian enclaves to leafy streets with all the laid-back ambience of old Europe. The city's motto says it all: Diversity our Strength.

An air of enthusiasm pervades the city. Downtown is populated by a mix of dynamic business people and laid-back individals, but they all share a common desire for their city to be best (and preferably first) at everything. This extends to their "green" credentials, the size and quality of their museums and galleries, the plethora of home-grown talent in arts and entertainment, and the achievements of their scientists and academics. It's the reason, perhaps, why Google chose it as the site for its projected "future city", to be built on a currently undeveloped 5ha (12-acre) waterfront site east of downtown. With all manner of innovative "smart" and green technology, the plan, subject to approval, will include a mix of residential and business developments.

Toronto has many attractions, but to get a real feel for the city it's just as important simply to hang out on a restaurant patio, on the lakeshore, or at one of the hundreds of festivals or free concerts.

FACTS AND FIGURES

● Toronto is on the same latitude as the French Riviera.
● Nearly half of Toronto's 2.7 million population were born outside of Canada.
● Toronto has more than 600km (373 miles) of cycling trails.
● Around 13 percent of Toronto consists of parkland, totaling some 8,000 ha (nearly 20,000 acres).

INSIDER INFORMATION

There's nothing like visiting a city with someone who knows their way around it, as they usually know all the best places to go, but if you don't have a friend in Toronto, don't despair. The Toronto Greeters Program provides (for free) a knowledgeable local to guide you around and share some of their own city secrets. Call 416/338-2786 for information.

HOLLYWOOD NORTH

Numerous movies and TV shows are filmed in Toronto. Popular locations include the Distillery Historic District (*Chicago, Cinderella Man, Suits*) and Casa Loma (the interior of the X-Men's "school for gifted youngsters"). City Hall was in both the new *Star Trek* and *The Handmaid's Tale*, which also included scenes in Ripley's Aquarium of Canada and a subway platform.

A RECORD LOST

For more than 30 years Toronto's CN Tower ruled supreme as the tallest free-standing building in the world, but in 2010 it was knocked into third place by the Burj Khalifa in Dubai (at 829.8m/2,722ft) and the Canon Tower in China (at 600m/1,969ft). The CN Tower stands at 553.3m (1,815.5ft) but has now dropped to ninth place.

A Short Stay in Toronto

DAY 1

Morning You might as well start out with a visit to the **CN Tower** (▷ 26–27) or it will constantly beckon from wherever else you are in the city. Arrive in good time for the 9am opening, and go all the way to the top for a spectacular view of Toronto.

Mid-morning Walk west along Front Street to Spadina, then take a streetcar north to Dundas to visit the spectacular **Art Gallery of Ontario** (AGO, ▷ 24–25), a showcase of both art and architecture.

Lunch Lunch at the AGO for a fine dining experience within the Frank Gehry extension on Dundas Street. Canadian art adorns the walls and local Canadian produce is on the menu. For a lighter meal, the café downstairs is equally good.

Afternoon Take the streetcar back down Spadina all the way to the lake-shore, then stroll east to take the ferry to **Toronto Islands** (▷ 66–67). Rent a bicycle or just stroll through the parkland, relax on one of the sandy beaches and perhaps take a dip in the lake.

Dinner Dress up and head to **Canoe** (▷ 59; 54th Floor TD Bank Tower, 66 Wellington Street West; tel 416/364-0054). This is one of Canada's finest restaurants, with excellent food and superb views, so make sure you have a reservation.

Evening Take in a Broadway-style show, concert or comedy night, then join the after-theater crowd at any place in the Entertainment District that appeals. The choice there includes chic cocktail lounges, pubs, jazz clubs and dance clubs, and you can just stroll until you see (or hear) something you like.

DAY 2

Morning Pick up a typical Toronto breakfast of a peameal bacon sandwich at **St. Lawrence Market** (▷ 51), then walk west along Front Street to Union Station and take the subway up to the Museum stop to visit the **Royal Ontario Museum** (ROM, ▷ 82–83).

Mid-morning After the museum, walk north across Bloor Street to explore the many upscale stores on the leafy streets of **Bloor-Yorkville** (▷ 84).

Lunch Le Paradis Restaurant (166 Bedford Road, tel 416/921-0995; lunch served Tue–Fri only) is a chic brasserie/bistro with a good-value fixed-price lunch.

Afternoon Take the subway to Dupont, then walk up to visit **Casa Loma** (▷ 80). Later, go to Greektown to stroll along Danforth Avenue to soak up the European atmosphere of this vibrant neighborhood.

Dinner Stay in Greektown to dine in style at the renowned **Pan on the Danforth restaurant** (516 Danforth Avenue, tel 416/466-8158, reservations advised), where traditional Mediterranean dishes are on the menu and the superb wine list offers a worldwide selection, including some unusual Greek choices.

Evening After dining, head back downtown for late-night live music at **Massey Hall** (▷ 58). It's a National Historic Site that's also full of rock 'n' roll and with a great ambience that often attracts big-name musicians. Alternatively, another great night out is to see the 10.30 show at **Second City** comedy club (▷ 38), Friday or Saturday only, both in the Entertainment District.

ESSENTIAL TORONTO TOP 25

▶ ▶ ▶

Art Gallery of Ontario
▷ 24–25 One of Canada's principal art galleries, strong on Canadian art.

Bata Shoe Museum
▷ 78–79 Fascinating collection of shoes through the ages.

Black Creek Pioneer Village ▷ 94 A complete small rural community replicating Victorian Ontario.

Yonge-Dundas Square
▷ 52–53 Soak up the buzzing atmosphere of downtown's hub.

Toronto Zoo ▷ 102 Animals from every continent roam spacious enclosures that try to re-create their natural habitats.

Toronto Islands ▷ 66–67 These peaceful islands with sandy beaches are just a short ferry ride away from downtown.

St. Lawrence Market
▷ 51 This historic market building offers a wonderful assortment of food.

Ripley's Aquarium of Canada ▷ 31 Get up close to sharks, rays and more.

Royal Ontario Museum
▷ 82–83 Canada's largest museum contains 6 million objects, including a superb collection of Chinese art.

Queen Street West
▷ 32 Vibrant area with trendy clothing stores galore, plus lively patios, bars and cafés.

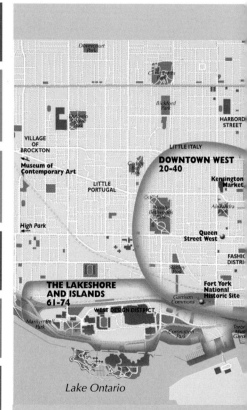

Ontario Science Centre
▷ 100–101 Nine superb exhibition halls packed with interactive displays.

Museum of Contemporary Art
▷ 98–99 Admire the new venue for modern art.

8

These pages are a quick guide to the Top 25, which are described in more detail later. Here they are listed alphabetically, and the tinted background shows which area they are in.

Canada's Wonderland
▷ 95 Canada's premier theme park, with 200 attractions.

Casa Loma ▷ 80
An 18th-century fairy-tale castle built for an early-20th-century millionaire.

City Hall ▷ 44–45
Instantly recognizable, the futuristic-looking City Hall was designed in the 1920s.

The CN Tower ▷ 26–27
An iconic building with one of the world's highest viewing platforms.

Design Exchange ▷ 46–47 Graceful Moderne building now dedicated to Canadian design.

Distillery District ▷ 48–49 Former distillery buildings now given over to culture.

Fort York ▷ 28–29
Historic spot where the city was founded in 1793.

Gardiner Museum ▷ 81
Superb museum with lots to see devoted to ceramic art, from pre-Columbian to the present.

Harbourfront Centre ▷ 64–65 Docklands, now revitalized as a commercial, cultural and leisure center.

High Park ▷ 96 Explore Toronto's largest city park's wild and cultivated areas.

McMichael Canadian Art Collection ▷ 97
Influential works of the Group of Seven artists.

Kensington Market
▷ 30 The perfect place to experience Toronto's vibrant multiculturalism.

Hockey Hall of Fame
▷ 50 A shrine to Canada's sporting obsession, with interactive exhibits.

Shopping

If you love to shop, come to Toronto with a fat wallet and a spare suitcase. The possibilities are seemingly endless, and you could shop every day for a month and still not discover all the quirky backstreet boutiques, cutting-edge products and highly individual craftworks.

From Malls to Markets

Among the particular pleasures of shopping here are the ease of getting around and the friendly staff. Add to this the delightful neighborhoods with specialty stores, the number of glittering malls and the traditional markets and you've got something really special. Even in the Financial District, the skyscraper towers often harbor one or more floors of shopping options at street level.

Fashion

Most of the world's top names in fashion have found a home in Toronto but some exciting home-grown designers are worth seeking out too. Holt Renfrew, at the heart of Bloor Street, is a good place to start for designs by Stephen Wong and Kirk Pickersgill, Laura Siegel, Chloe and Parris Gordon, and Kimberley Newport-Mimran. Sid Neigum's stunning geometric creations are available at Room @ The Bay, at Yonge and Queen Street, and at Jonathan+Olivia at 49 Ossington Avenue. Diamonds, watches and crystal sparkle at Tiffany's, Royal de Versailles, Cartier and Swarovski. Roots Canada, a giant in casual clothing and sportswear, occupies a large space.

SOMETHING OLD

Amid all the modernity, things from the past have a special appeal, and you'll find classy antiques on Davenport Road at Avenue, along King Street, and at the Sunday Antique Market on The Esplanade. Even more fascinating is The Salvage Shop on Kingston Road, with its huge array of decidedly unclassy items, from household goods and tools to old typewriters and tailors' dummies.

Top to bottom:
St. Lawrence Market;
shopping in Toronto's
busy stores and malls;

Arts and Crafts

Toronto's arts and crafts communities show their works on Queen Street West, which abounds with custom jewelers, sophisticated glass sculpture galleries, and native and Inuit art. St. Lawrence Market hosts local vendors selling their own craftwork, and the Arts Market has original art and a variety of crafts at its three stores in the city—two on Queen Street East (at Nos 790 and 1114) and another at 846 College Street.

Music

Toronto is proud of its musicians and entertainers, and the huge HMV store on Yonge Street stages live in-store performances. Most Toronto music stores dedicate shelves to Canadian-bred talent such as The Tragically Hip, Drake, Rush and The Weeknd.

Historic Stores

At Queen's Quay Terminal the Tilley Endurables Shop features the Tilley Hat. Advertised with the story of one having been retrieved intact after it was eaten by an elephant, each Tilley Hat comes with a lifetime guarantee and owner's manual. The Hudson's Bay Company, a former fur trading post that's as old as Canada itself, and now known simply as Hudson's Bay, is a major store selling everything from fashion and home furnishing to appliances and electronics. You will also find a superb range of stores on Bloor and Yonge, as well as a selection in suburban shopping malls.

Kensington market;
Yonge-Dundas Square

PICK UP A BARGAIN

There is nothing so satisfying as finding a real bargain, and the best time for this in Toronto is the first day of business after Christmas, when prices are routinely slashed by half (or more). There are sales in summer, too, roughly June through August. Year-round bargains can be found in the out-of-city discount malls, such as Dixie Outlet Mall at Mississauga, Vaughan Mills at Concord and Toronto Premium Outlets on 401 toward Milton.

Shopping by Theme

Whether you're looking for a department store, a quirky boutique or something in between, you'll find it all in Toronto. On this page shops are listed by theme. For a more detailed write-up, see the individual listings in Toronto by Area.

Antiques
Abraham's (▷ 35)
Toronto Antiques on King (▷ 36)

Arts and Crafts
Bay of Spirits Gallery (▷ 57)
Bergo Designs (▷ 57)
The Centre Shop (▷ 71)
Craft Ontario (▷ 89)
ESP (Erin Stump Projects) (▷ 35)
Lakeview Market (▷ 71)
The Power Plant (▷ 71)
William Ashley (▷ 87)

Books and Toys
The Beguiling Books & Art (▷ panel, 36)
Ben McNally Books (▷ panel, 36, 57)
Book City (▷ panel, 36)
Rolo (▷ 87)

Clothes for Men
8th and Main (▷ 57)
Gotstyle (▷ 36)
Harry Rosen (▷ 87)
Haven (▷ 57)
M0851 (▷ 87)

Clothes for Women
8th and Main (▷ 57)
Club Monaco (▷ 35)
Freda's (▷ 35)
Fresh Collective (▷ 35)
Holt Renfrew Centre (▷ 87)
John Fluevog (▷ 36)
Kumari's (▷ 87)
Lavish and Squalor (▷ 36)
M0851 (▷ 87)

Food and Drink
Kitchen Table (▷ 71)
LCBO (▷ 71)
Pusateri's Fine Foods (▷ 87)
Ten Ren Tea (▷ 36)

Homewares
Bookhou (▷ 35)
Drake General Store (▷ 35)

Jewelry
Anne Sportun Fine Jewellery (▷ 35)
Corktown Designs (▷ 57)
Silverbridge (▷ 87)

Malls/Department Stores
Holt Renfrew (▷ panel, 57, 87)
Harry Rosen (▷ 87)
Hudson's Bay (▷ panel, 57)
Queen's Quay Terminal (▷ 71)
CF Toronto Eaton Centre (▷ 57)
Yorkville Village Shopping Centre (▷ 87)

Music
Grigorian (▷ 87)
Sonic Boom (▷ 36)

Sports
Mountain Equipment Co-op (MEC) (▷ 36)
Real Sports Apparel (▷ 57)

Toronto by Night

Toronto is as lively by night as it is during the day. As well as the theater district (▷ below), there are world-class concert halls, stadium rock concerts at the Rogers Centre, the Scotiabank Arena (formerly the Air Canada Centre), or the Budweiser Stage at Ontario Place, all atmospheric live venues that leave no musical stone unturned, and a huge choice of clubs and bars.

Clubs, Clubs and More Clubs

Many of the city's dance clubs are on the Richmond Street strip just south of Queen West, which is in itself home to a number of the live music venues. King Street West, known for upscale clubs serving cocktails to a sophisticated clientele, has lively party venues too. The College Street area is also a good bet for up-and-coming dance bars, though the area, with its many cafés and bistros, is more oriented toward a laid-back lounge crowd. When the clubs close (by 3am) night owls seek out all-night raves publicized only by word of mouth.

Live Music

Canadian musicians often become international stars, and many honed their talents in Toronto's live music venues. A night out could give you a preview of the next chart-topper. The entertainment district is a hotbed of music from rock to jazz to salsa, and rappers to singer-songwriters. Start with a walk along Bloor, Queen West or College, then just follow your ears.

THEATRE DISTRICT

Since the mid-19th century, the area now known as the Theatre District has been animated with music halls, theaters and entertainment palaces. With around a dozen theaters, it offers world-class productions. The opening of the Royal Alexandra Theatre in 1907 breathed life into the area, and when, in the 1960s, it was threatened with demolition, Toronto businessman Ed Mirvish saved and restored it, sparking Mirvish Productions, which now owns and operates several of the city's finest theaters.

Top to bottom: City Hall; patrons enjoying a drink in a downtown bar; Chinatown

Where to Eat

Toronto is reputed to have no fewer than 7,000 restaurants, and though these include fast-food joints and neighborhood diners, you are still spoiled for choice with really excellent places to eat. This cosmopolitan city encompasses just about every major culture in its cuisine and prides itself on being Canada's trendsetter.

Neighborhood Dining

The famous neighborhoods of Toronto make it easy to find a particular cuisine: Little Italy and Corso Italia; Greektown on the Danforth; Little India; Koreatown; Portugal Village; Little Poland; and a choice of Chinatowns. Shopping neighborhoods, such as Bloor-Yorkville, Yonge Street and the Fashion District, have plenty of eateries, and the Entertainment District is full of places offering pre- and post-show dinners. You can even join the power breakfast set in a Financial District eatery. If you happen upon a place where the locals go, you are guaranteed the best food and a great atmosphere.

Food Festivals

The best times to sample the various cuisines in Toronto is during one of the national-themed festivals: Chinese New Year (Jan/Feb); Taste of Little Italy (Jun); Toronto Caribbean Carnival, Taste of the Danforth, Festival of South Asia and MuslimFest in Mississauga (Jul/Aug); and the Bloor West Village Toronto Ukrainian Festival and the Hispanic Fiesta (early Sep). Canadian food is on offer at the Canadian National Exhibition (mid-Aug/early Sep) and the Royal Agricultural Winter Fair (Nov).

TAKE TO THE LAKE

Try a brunch, lunch or dinner cruise. Prices are $45–$90, and some include dancing. Try Mariposa Cruises (tel 416/203-0178, mariposacruises.com); Cruise Toronto (tel 416/260-6355; cruisetoronto.com); Jubilee Queen (tel 416/203-7245, jubileequeencruises.ca); or Great Lakes Schooner (tel: 416/260-6355, greatlakesschooner.com).

Top to bottom:
Chinatown by day;
Chinatown food; freshly
baked bread; alfresco
dining in Little Italy

Where to Eat by Cuisine

There are plenty of places to eat to suit all tastes and budgets in Toronto. On this page they are listed by cuisine. For a more detailed description of each venue, see Toronto by Area.

African
The Sultan's Tent & Café Moroc (▷ 60)

Chinese
Dumpling House Restaurant (▷ 39)
Wah Sing (▷ 40)

Continental
Adega (▷ 59)
Alexandros Take-Out (▷ 74)
Chiado (▷ 39)
Esplanade Bier Markt (▷ 59)
Future Bistro (▷ 90)
Scaramouche (▷ panel, 40)

Diner Fare
The Carousel Café (▷ 74)
Fran's (▷ 59)
Urban Eatery (▷ panel, 60)

Eclectic/Fusion
Fred's Not Here (▷ 40)
Matahari (▷ 40)

French
Bymark (▷ 59)
Le Sélect Bistro (▷ 40)
Osgoode Hall Restaurant (▷ 60)

Italian
Café Diplomatico (▷ 39)
Fieramosca (▷ 90)
Fusaro's Italian Kitchen (▷ 40)

Japanese
Ema-Tei (▷ 40)
Nami (▷ 59)
Wow Sushi (▷ 90)

Mexican
Como en Casa (▷ 90)

North American
360 at the CN Tower (▷ 39, panel, 40)
City Kitchen (▷ panel, 60)
Canoe (▷ panel, 40, 59)
Museum Tavern (▷ 90)
Senator (▷ 60)
Tundra (▷ 60)

Pub and Bar Food
Amsterdam Brewhouse (▷ 74)
Irish Embassy Pub & Grill (▷ 59)
Roof Lounge (▷ panel, 40)

Seafood
Joso's (▷ 90)
Pearl Diver (▷ 60)

Steaks/Grills
Pearl Harbourfront Restaurant (▷ 74)
Harbour Sixty Steakhouse (▷ 74)
Morton's (▷ 90)
Ruth's Chris Steak House (▷ 60)

Top Tips For...

These great suggestions will help you tailor your ideal visit to Toronto, no matter how you choose to spend your time. Each sight or listing has a fuller write-up elsewhere in the book.

A MEAL WITH A VIEW

Splash out on a meal at 360 (▷ 39) and soak up the views of the entire city as you revolve a full circle high up on the CN Tower.

Pick out a prime spot on a patio at the Pearl Harbourfront Restaurant (▷ 74) at Queen's Quay Terminal (▷ 69) and watch all the activity on the lake.

Get room service at the Renaissance Toronto Downtown hotel and watch a ball game from a room overlooking the Rogers Centre stadiums pitch (▷ 33).

Reserve a window seat at Canoe (▷ 59) and look down over the Financial District while savoring upscale Canadian cuisine.

CUTTING-EDGE CULTURE

Check out what's on at the Buddies in Bad Times Theatre (▷ 88), which stages productions that challenge social boundaries.

Explore unconventional works on display at the new Museum of Contemporary Art (▷ 98–99).

Find out what came top in the annual awards at the Design Exchange (▷ 46–47).

Historic it may be, but the Distillery District (▷ 48–49) has a lively program of unusual shows and events, from the Toronto Alternative Arts and Fashion Week to up-and-coming bands and innovative arts and crafts.

TORONTO FOR FREE

Watch the street performers and parades at Yonge-Dundas Square (▷ 52–53).

Celebrity spot on Queen Street West (▷ 32).

Go behind the scenes at CBC Broadcasting Centre's museum (▷ 33).

Center yourself at the public labyrinth (▷ 55).

Clockwise from top left: Rogers Centre; cyclists on the Toronto Islands; an art exhibition in the

FRESH AIR AND EXERCISE

Rent a bicycle and pedal around the Toronto Islands (▷ 66–67).

Skim across Lake Ontario in a boat rented from the Harbourfront Centre Sailing and Power-boating (▷ 65).

Take the subway to High Park (▷ 96) and hike through the natural forest of the Spring Creek and West Ravine nature trails.

Admire the lake at The Beaches (▷ 103) or Toronto Islands (▷ 66–67).

Sign up, if you can, for a keeper-for-the-day program at Toronto Zoo (▷ 102); otherwise there's plenty of walking around the spacious enclosures.

INSIDE INFORMATION

Lectures by experts open up new insights at the Royal Ontario Museum (▷ 82–83).

The Ontario Science Centre (▷ 100–101) occasionally hosts presentations by members of the Royal Astronomical Society of Canada.

Head for St. Lawrence Market (▷ 51) any Saturday at noon for demonstrations by chefs and food experts, preceded by a short talk about the history of the market (in the South Market building).

Find out what the provincial government is up to by watching parliament in session at the Ontario Legislature (▷ 84).

A LAID-BACK AFTERNOON

Linger over a cappuccino and cake at Café Diplomatico (▷ 39) and absorb the atmosphere of Little Italy (▷ 33).

Escape the bustle of Yonge Street and savor the peaceful haven of the Allan Gardens (▷ 54).

Take a picnic to the Toronto Islands (▷ 66–67) and laze away the afternoon on the beach or under a shady tree.

Stretch out on the grass at the peaceful Toronto Music Garden (▷ 69) with its sculptural curves and undulations, perhaps further soothed by an open-air recital.

Distillery District; a blues concert; Hanlan's Point on Toronto Islands; Ontario Legislature

GREAT LIVE MUSIC

Check out Massey Hall (▷ 58). Built in 1894, this National Historic Site has had many famous faces appear on its stage, and it continues to be one of Toronto's finest concert venues for music of all types.

Celebrity connections (Alex Lifeson of Rush) guarantee top-notch rock, jazz, funk and R&B at the Orbit Room (▷ 38).

Known for showcasing future stars from home and abroad, the Horseshoe Tavern (▷ 37) is a Toronto institution.

Chill out to the folk/acoustic performers in the intimate C'Est What cellar bar (▷ 58).

Catch an open-air world music show on the Concert Stage at the Harbourfront Centre (▷ 65).

Join the crowds for a megastar concert at the the Rogers Centre (▷ 33).

WINDOW SHOPPING

Browse the dozen traders at Toronto Antiques on King (▷ 36) for treasures that would never fit in a suitcase.

Stroll around chic Bloor-Yorkville (▷ 84) with its array of upscale designer boutiques—Prada, Chanel, Gucci, et al—and see where the celebrities come to shop.

Wander along Queen Street West (▷ 32) for cutting-edge Canadian fashion designers as well as international couturiers.

Drool over the superstar designer footwear at John Fluevog (▷ 36).

ENTERTAIN THE KIDS

Cheer on the jousting knights and admire the regal falcons at a Toronto Castle show (▷ 72).

Discover some fancy footwork at Baha Shoe Museum (▷ 78–79).

Go up, down and round and round at Canada's Wonderland (▷ 95).

Discover natural wonders at High Park on a family walk or at a crafting activity (▷ 96).

Walk under the water at Ripley's Aquarium of Canada (▷ 31).

Top to bottom: Toronto's music and shopping options sum up the city's great variety

Toronto by Area

Downtown West

This area buzzes with creative energy: in the theaters and concert halls of the Entertainment District, in the design houses of the Fashion District and in the art galleries. The CN Tower is an icon of architectural creativity—and you might see sporting creativity in the Rogers Centre.

LITTLE ITALY

Street labels (top section, left to right):
Street · Avenue · Boulevard · Avenue

Crace Street · Clinton Street · Manning Avenue · Euclid Avenue · Palmerston Boulevard · Markham Street · BATHURST STREET · Uppincott Street · Vankoughnet Street · Borden Street

COLLEGE STREET

Gore Street
Henderson Street
Cinder Ave · Clinton Avenue
Mansfield Avenue

Harrison Street · Crawford Street · Montrose Avenue · Beatrice Street · Crace Street · Bellwoods Avenue · Claremont Street · Manning Avenue · Euclid Avenue · Palmerston Boulevard · Markham Street

Nassau Street
Toronto Western Hospital
Leonard Avenue
Wales

Uppincott Street

DUNDAS STREET WEST

Halton Street

Shaw Street · Crawford Street

Bellwoods Place
Bellwoods Avenue · Manning Avenue · Euclid Avenue · Palmerston Boulevard · Markham Street

Trinity Bellwoods Park

Alexandra Park

Argyle Street
Lobb Avenue

Shaw Street · Crawford Street · Gore Vale Avenue · Bellwoods Avenue · Gore Street · Claremont Street

Robinson Street
Carr Street

Theatre Passe Muraille
Ryerson Avenue

Trinity Community Recreation Centre

Manning Avenue
Crocker Avenue
Wolseley Street · Willis Street
Wolseley Street

QUEEN STREET WEST

BATHURST STREET

QUEEN

Richmond Street · Walnut Avenue · Richmond Street West · Richmond
Mitchell Avenue

Shaw Street · Crawford Street · Massey Street · STRACHAN AVENUE · Stafford Street · Terrace · Stanley Street · Walnut Avenue · Niagara Street · Tecumseth Street · Portugal Square

Factory Theatre

Artword Theatre & Gallery
Portland Street

Adelaide Street · Adelaide Street West

Shank Street
Whitaker Avenue · Michener Crescent

KING STREET WEST

KING

Caniff Street
Douro Street

Stanley Park

Stewart Street

Victoria Memorial Park

Wellington Street West

Niagara Street

FRONT

Garrison Commons

Fort York National Historic Site

Dan Leckie Way

FREDERICK

GARDINER

0 ___ 250 m
0 ___ 250 yds

N

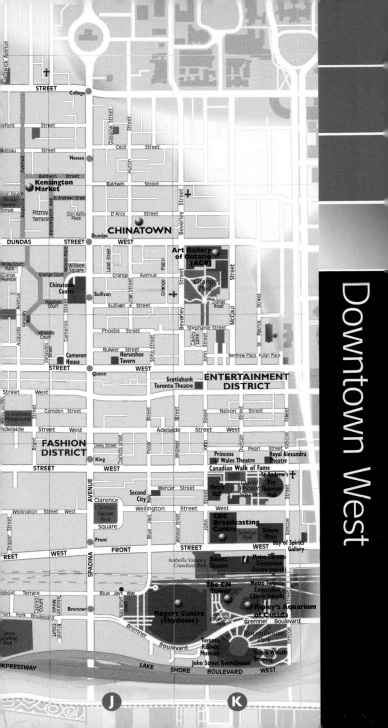

STREET

College

xford   Street

Nassau   Street

Glasgow Street

Cecil   Street

Huron   Street

Baldwin   Street

Kensington Market

St Andrews Street

Fitzroy Terrace

Glen Baillie Place

Baldwin   Street

D'Arcy   Street

Beverley Street

CHINATOWN

DUNDAS   STREET   WEST

Dundas

Art Gallery of Ontario (AGO)

Willison Square

Larch Street

Grange   Avenue

Chinatown Centre

Grange Park

Grange Road

Sullivan

Sullivan   Street

Huron Street

McCaul   Street

St Patrick   Street

Vanauley Court

Phoebe   Street

Stephanie Street

Bulwer   Street

Horseshoe Tavern

Soho Street

Carey's Lane

John   Street

Renfrew Place   Pullan Place

Cameron House

STREET   WEST

Queen

Scotiabank Toronto Theatre

ENTERTAINMENT DISTRICT

Street   West

Camden   Street

Nelson   Street

St Andrews Street

Adelaide   Street   West

Adelaide   Street   West

FASHION DISTRICT

Oxley Street

Charlotte Street

Widmer   Street

Peter   Street

Duncan   Street

Pearl   Street

Simcoe   Street

King

STREET   WEST

Princess of Wales Theatre

Royal Alexandra Theatre

Canadian Walk of Fame

St Andrew's

Mercer Street

Second City

Metro Hall

David Pecaut Square

Roy Thomson Hall

Clarence

Clarence Square Park

Square

Wellington   Street   West

Wellington   Street

CBC Broadcasting Centre

Simcoe Park

Simcoe Place

Draper   Street

Front

FRONT   STREET   WEST

Blue Jays Way

Windsor Street

Bay of Spirits Gallery

REET   WEST

Isabella Valancy Crawford Park

Budweiser Theatre

Metro Toronto Convention Centre (north)

SPADINA AVENUE

eboat   Terrace

Telegram Mews

Bremner

Blue Jays Way

The CN Tower

Metro Toronto Convention Centre (south)

ort York Boulevard

Rogers Centre (Skydome)

Ripley's Aquarium of Canada

Bremner   Boulevard

Roundhouse Park

ranue nding Park

Brunel Court

Bremner   Boulevard

Toronto Railway Museum

Steam Whistle Brewing

KPRESSWAY

LAKE   SHORE

John Street Roundhouse

BOULEVARD   WEST

Downtown West

J   K

Art Gallery of Ontario

HIGHLIGHTS

● *Corpus* (Bernini)
● *The Massacre of the Innocents* (Rubens)
● *The Fire in the Saint-Jean Quarter, Seen Looking Westward* (Joseph Légaré)
● *West Wind* (Tom Thomson)

TIP

● The AGO restaurant is a cut above the usual museum café. It offers fine dining from a skilled chef, and ingredients sourced from sustainable farming.

Within a stunning contemporary building that is itself a joy to behold, the Art Gallery of Ontario (AGO) is one of North America's finest and largest treasure-houses of art. Its collections span the globe and the ages.

The setting The soaring 200m (600ft) curved glass frontage along Dundas Street cannot fail to entice passersby, with its views into a sculpture gallery that's flooded with natural light. The four-story titanium and glass south wing also benefits from the daylight that streams through its glass roof. Elsewhere, windowless galleries are artfully lit to draw the eye toward the exhibits, benches invite quiet contemplation, and art spills into non-gallery spaces, making use of every suitable wall space.

Clockwise from left: Cherub fountain outside the Ontario Art Gallery; children playing among some exhibits; the stunning glass frontage designed by Frank Gehry; interior of the light-filled gallery

Collections The gallery has a total collection of around 80,000 works, covering many periods, genres and parts of the world. It also has a lively schedule of events, educational programs and community projects. The Canadian galleries range from First Nations art to the Group of Seven to innovative contemporary artists. There are also important European works—the 17th-century collection is outstanding—with works by Van Gogh, Picasso, Chagall, Modigliani, Gaugin, the surrealists and others, while the African and Australian Aboriginal art collection is the best in North America. The AGO also houses the world's largest collection of Henry Moore works, with plaster and bronze maquettes. You can hear recordings of Moore discussing his work and his affection for Toronto, and see some of the items that inspired him.

THE BASICS

ago.net

✚ K5

✉ 317 Dundas Street West

☎ 416/979-6648

🕐 Tue–Sun 10–5.30 (Wed and Fri till 9)

🍴 Restaurant (tel 416/979-6688), café

Ⓢ St. Patrick

🚌 505 Dundas streetcar

♿ Very good

💰 Moderate

❓ Tours, lectures, films, youth activities

The CN Tower

HIGHLIGHTS

- Glass Floor
- SkyPod
- EdgeWalk
- The ride up

TIP

- Instead of rushing to the tower in the morning, wait until evening, head for the SkyPod and stay to watch the sun go down and the city lights go on. It's quite a sight.

The CN Tower, 553.3m (1,815ft) high, is Toronto's trademark building. It was derided at first but ultimately embraced by citizens. Until 2010, it was the world's tallest building, but then a 829.8m (2,722ft) Dubai hotel overtook it. Now a building boom in China has pushed it into ninth place.

Unrivaled views It's certainly a stomach-churning experience to rocket up at 3m (10ft) per second in glass-fronted elevators to the Look Out level, where there are breathtaking views through floor-to-ceiling windows. Here you can stand—if you dare—on the Glass Floor, 342m (1,122ft) above the ground, then step onto the Outdoor Sky Terrace. On a clear day, you can see the mist of Niagara Falls across the

Clockwise from left: the tower looms from below; on the EdgeWalk; the tower's distinctive silhouette is striking even at night; the view from the SkyPod window

lake, though the safety netting detracts a little. Take the elevator another 33 stories up to the SkyPod at 447m (1,465ft). For an uninterrupted view, by reservation, you can take the EdgeWalk, where, safely harnessed, you can stroll around, and even lean out from a 1.5m (5-foot) ledge atop the tower's main pod. The tower has attracted record-seekers—including the multi world-record holder Ashrita Furman, who bounced on his pogo stick up the 1,899 steps to the LookOut roof in 57 minutes and 51 seconds. An annual stairclimb attracts thousands of entrants, who raise money for charity.

Shopping and other entertainments Down at the base of the tower there's an arcade with techno games and simulator rides, and the Marketplace offers varied shopping.

THE BASICS

cntower.ca

✚ K8

✉ 301 Front Street West

☎ 416/868-6937

🕐 Tower daily 9am–10.30pm. Other attractions vary

🍴 360 Restaurant, tel 416/362-5411, Le Café

🚇 Union

🚌 510 Spadina streetcar

♿ Very good

✋ Observation deck expensive; EdgeWalk expensive; games expensive

27

Fort York National Historic Site

HIGHLIGHTS

● Officers' Quarters
● Stone Magazine
● Artillery demonstrations

TIP

● Visit during July and August, when well-drilled, uniformed students perform guard drills, artillery demonstrations, military music and drumming.

This complex of buildings, sandwiched between the railroad tracks and the highway, will give you a historic jolt back to 1813 when York, as Toronto was then known, was a muddy, rough-and-ready imperial outpost.

Toronto's historic birthplace The Fort York National Historic Site is the birthplace of modern urban Toronto and has the largest collection of 1812-era military structures in the country. The visitor center (opened in 2014) has been sensitively designed to blend into the historic site. Exhibits include rarely or never-seen-before historical objects, such as war service uniforms and Canadian-made rifles, as well as contemporary art featuring the war of 1812 and the battle of 1813.

Clockwise from left: Costumed interpreters against a modern backdrop; a bird's eye view of the site; live demonstrations help visitors to imagine life in the fort during the 19th century; cannons defend the walls

Fort York and the White House On April 27, 1813, 2,700 Americans stormed ashore from Lake Ontario, drove out the troops at Fort York and set fire to Government House and the Parliament Buildings. In 1814, in retaliation, the British occupied Washington and burned the president's residence. Canadian legend says it was renamed the White House after the blackened walls were covered with white paint, but the Americans say it was named for the color of the stone.

Historic walls John Graves Simcoe built a garrison on the site of Fort York in 1793. The fort was strengthened in 1811 (the west wall and circular battery date from that time) and, shortly after the events of 1813, the British rebuilt it; most of the fort's buildings date from then.

THE BASICS

toronto.ca/culture
forkyork.ca
✚ G8
✉ Garrison Road, off Lakeshore Boulevard
☎ 416/392-6907
🕑 Victoria Day–Labour Day daily 10–5; rest of year Mon–Fri 10–4, Sat–Sun 10–5. May be closed for special events
🚋 511 Bathurst streetcar
♿ Few
💲 Inexpensive
❓ Tours by interpreters in costume

Kensington Market

Colorful shops and goods for sale at Kensington Market

THE BASICS

kensington-market.ca

🚻 H5

✉ Bounded by Spadina Avenue and Bathurst Street and College and Dundas streets

🕐 Stores 11–7 (food stores open earlier)

🚌 505 Dundas, 506 College, 510 Spadina or 511 Bathurst streetcars

HIGHLIGHTS

● Blue Banana Market
● Global Cheese
● Segovia Meats
● My Market Bakery
● Caribbean Corner
● Casa Acoreana
● Essence of Life Organics

Colorful, quirky, a riot of street sounds and tempting aromas… this National Historic Site offers authentic shopping in a multi-ethnic hub. It's where locals congregate and visitors come to enjoy the uplifting atmosphere.

Tastes of the world Culinary delights are the major draw here, but don't expect to find a central market square—there is just a series of narrow streets with stores selling a colorful array of food. Wander along Kensington and Augusta avenues and Baldwin Street for West Indian grocery stores full of sugar cane, plantains, yucca and the like, and for delicatessens, fresh fish stores and artisan cheeses from around the world. Augusta and Baldwin have health foods aplenty, too.

Street vibe Food and history aside, there is an edgy, up-to-the-minute feel about the place, with a lot of young fashion designers selling in the market boutiques (such as Fresh Collective, ▷ 35), and individuals combing the stores to create their own look, often with a vintage element. There's a café culture here, too, with people chilling out and visitors lingering over their coffee and drinking in the scene. There's a wide range of restaurants, bars and coffee shops to choose from, many with patios and outside tables, and some of them have live music in the evenings. A three-day jazz festival in mid-September sums up the artistic, musical and community ambiance.

Ripley's Aquarium of Canada

One of Toronto's most-visited family attractions, Ripley's Aquarium includes 57 live exhibits, four touch pools, more than 100 interactive exhibits, and six play areas for young visitors. Conveniently, it is located right next to the CN Tower.

Freshwater and saltwater This popular aquarium exhibits over 16,000 exotic specimens, from more than 450 species, organized into nine distinct galleries. The Canadian Waters gallery includes the giant Pacific octopus, wolf eels, lobsters and rockfish. One exhibit, not to be missed, simulates waves, with Pacific kelp calmly flowing through the surges.

The exhibitions The Rainbow Reef shows off the tropical species from the Indo-Pacific region and includes daily interactive dive shows. At the Dangerous Lagoon you'll move through an underwater tunnel while gazing up and around at sharks, stingrays, sawfish and the occasional green sea turtle. Some exhibits allow visitors to touch sharks, stingrays and horseshoe crabs. Mother Nature's Art Gallery is home to the world's most delicate species, such as the red lionfish, electric eel, lined seahorse and weedy sea dragon. The Ray Bay focuses on stingrays, which you can see being fed, while the Shoreline gallery gets you close to sharks. The Life Support Systems gallery allows visitors to get a behind-the-scenes look into the workings of the aquarium's vital life-support and filtration equipment.

THE BASICS

ripleyaquariums.com

➕ K8

✉ 288 Bremner Boulevard

☎ 647/351-3474

🕐 Daily 9am–11pm

🍴 Ripley's Café

🚇 510 Spadina streetcar

♿ Good

💲 Expensive

HIGHLIGHTS

● Spotting the giant Pacific octopus
● Close-ups with sharks and stingrays
● Dangerous Lagoon underwater tunnel

TIP

● Purchase tickets online in advance of your visit to avoid long lines for the limited number of walk-up tickets.

Queen Street West

TOP 25

The historic red-brick frontages that characterize this popular street

THE BASICS

✚ J6

✉ Queen Street West between Bathurst and Simcoe

🍴 Restaurants, cafés and snackbars

🚌 501 Queen streetcar

HIGHLIGHTS

● Queen Mother Café
● Scouting out vintage clothing treasures
● Celebrity spotting

Set against a backdrop of gorgeous and historic buildings, the Queen Street West neighborhood is one of Toronto's best shopping and dining areas, and is known as a centre for visual arts.

Beginnings Queen Street West runs along its namesake Queen Street between Bathurst and Simcoe and, during the 1960s and 1970s, it was well known as a hippy hangout with cheap rent and greasy spoon diners. During the 1980s it became the de facto nightclub strip and the music scene quickly churned out famous punk rockers and led to the popular MuchMusic (now Much) channel.

Arty crowd Soon after, the students from the nearby Ontario College of Art and Design (now called OCAD University) began to transform the Queen Street West neighborhood into a vibrant arts community. This popularized the area, increasing the living costs, and eventually changing it from a hippy hangout to the upscale haven it is today.

Toronto's Fashion District The area is now home to new designers, and an extensive array of shoe, fabric, bead and clothing stores border Queen Street West to the north, while the west of Queen Street West is dubbed gallery central. All along Queen Street you'll find patio-fronted cafés, trendy bars, excellent live music venues, fine-dining restaurants, and the occasional inexpensive diner too.

More to See

CBC BROADCASTING CENTRE

cbc.ca

This distinctive work of architecture with a colorful exterior is one of the largest broadcasting centers in North America. In the grand Barbara Frum Atrium, named for the distinguished Canadian journalist and designed by Philip Johnson, you can see radio hosts presenting shows and technicians keeping everyone on track. The space is 10 floors high and topped with a skylight. The little museum (capacity 50 people) is fun and free. Enjoy a variety of clips from radio and TV, and the interactive exhibits. Special exhibitions have included radio sound effects and props from popular kids' programs.

➕ K7 ✉ 250 Front Street West
☎ 416/205-5574 🕐 Mon–Fri 9–5
🍴 Cafeteria 🚇 Union 🚻 Good

CHINATOWN

Sprawling along Dundas and Spadina, the original Chinatown bustles day and night. People shop for green mustard and bok choy, fresh crabs and live fish, and herbal stores selling ginseng that costs hundreds of dollars for just one ounce. Restaurants are a big part of the attraction, while Chinese New Year, with dragon dances and drumming, is a highlight of the Toronto calendar.

➕ J5 ✉ St. Patrick 🚋 505 Dundas streetcar

LITTLE ITALY

littleitalycollegest.com

A vibrant Italian community thrives along College Street between Bathurst and Ossington, where the street lamps bear neon maps of Italy, and stretches north to Harbord and south to Dundas. Old-style cafés neighbor more fashionable establishments. At night, in particular, the area buzzes with energy as people flock to the restaurants.

➕ G3 🚋 506 Carlton streetcar

ROGERS CENTRE

rogerscentre.com

One of the largest Major League baseball stadiums ever built, a tour at the home of the Blue Jays takes visitors behind the scenes, including to the press box and a luxury suite. The stadium incorporates an 11-story hotel where some rooms have great views over the field and can be rented on game nights for upward of $300. Other entertainment includes truck racing, concerts and ice shows.

➕ K8 ✉ 1 Blue Jays Way ☎ 416/341-1000 🕐 Times vary, call ahead 🚇 Union 🚻 Good 🤚 Tours moderate

TRINITY BELLWOODS PARK

Toronto is known for its parks and, at more than 14 ha (35 acres), this is the largest downtown green space. It's a delightful place to have a picnic, but there's a lot going on here too, including various courts for sports, a children's playground and an ice rink. There's a farmers' market every Tuesday afternoon at the Dundas Street end and various events, including the annual Queen West Art Crawl in mid-September, which features a huge art exhibition and concerts.

➕ F5 ✉ 790 Queen Street West 🚋 501 Queen or 505 Dundas streetcar 🚻 Good 🤚 Free

Downtown West Highlights

Start with the city's best view, then tour theaterland and a couple of colorful neighborhoods, with the superb AGO along the way.

DISTANCE: 3km (1.8 miles) **ALLOW:** 2.5 hours

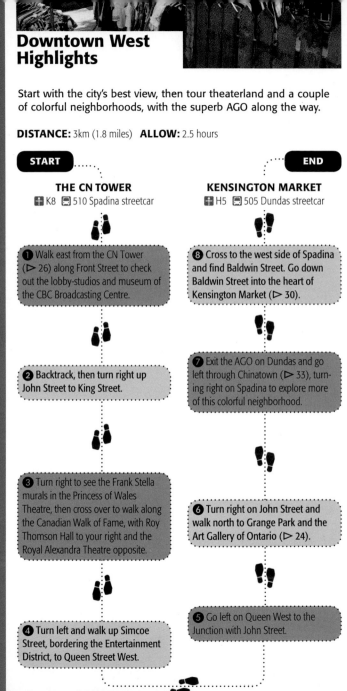

START

THE CN TOWER
⊞ K8 🚋 510 Spadina streetcar

① Walk east from the CN Tower (▷ 26) along Front Street to check out the lobby-studios and museum of the CBC Broadcasting Centre.

② Backtrack, then turn right up John Street to King Street.

③ Turn right to see the Frank Stella murals in the Princess of Wales Theatre, then cross over to walk along the Canadian Walk of Fame, with Roy Thomson Hall to your right and the Royal Alexandra Theatre opposite.

④ Turn left and walk up Simcoe Street, bordering the Entertainment District, to Queen Street West.

END

KENSINGTON MARKET
⊞ H5 🚋 505 Dundas streetcar

⑧ Cross to the west side of Spadina and find Baldwin Street. Go down Baldwin Street into the heart of Kensington Market (▷ 30).

⑦ Exit the AGO on Dundas and go left through Chinatown (▷ 33), turning right on Spadina to explore more of this colorful neighborhood.

⑥ Turn right on John Street and walk north to Grange Park and the Art Gallery of Ontario (▷ 24).

⑤ Go left on Queen West to the Junction with John Street.

DOWNTOWN WEST WALK

ABRAHAM'S

This may not be a high-end antiques store, but it is a cherry-picker's delight. The space is jammed to the ceiling with all kinds of curios and ephemera, from gas pumps to bicycles and neon beer signs to musical instruments.

H6 ✉ 635 Queen Street West
☎ 416/504-6210 ⏰ Mon–Fri 11–6, Sat 11–7
🚋 501 Queen streetcar

ANNE SPORTUN JEWELLERY

annesportun.com

Designer Anne Sportun uses traditional goldsmithing techniques to make striking pieces inspired by nature and the universal language of shape and symbol. Precious stones are set in rings, earrings, necklaces or pendants.

F7 ✉ 742 Queen Street West
☎ 416/363-4114 ⏰ Mon–Wed, Sat 11–6, Thu–Fri 11–7, Sun 12–5 🚋 501 Queen streetcar

BOOKHOU

bookhou.com

A local husband-and-wife design team create beautiful bags, pillow covers, children's clothing, pottery and furniture. They beautifully and esthetically incorporate natural materials such as linen, felt, canvas, clay and wood.

G5 ✉ 798 Dundas Street West
☎ 416/203-2549 ⏰ Tue–Sat 11–6 🚋 505 Dundas streetcar

CLUB MONACO

clubmonaco.ca

For casual, young fashions there is nowhere better than this chain, with several outlets in the city. This is the brand's original store.

H6 ✉ 403 Queen Street West
☎ 416/979-5633 ⏰ Mon–Sat 11–8, Sun 11–6
🚋 Queen Street West streetcar

DRAKE GENERAL STORE

drakegeneralstore.ca

Located across the street from the Drake Hotel, this shop sells intriguing curios and souvenirs that are definitively Canadian. Find local retro maps, Toronto-based Camp Skincare products, housemade teas, and a host of other gift ideas here.

D6 ✉ 1151 Queen Street West
☎ 647/346-0742 ⏰ Mon–Sat 10–9, Sun 11–6
🚋 501 Queen streetcar

ESP (ERIN STUMP PROJECTS)

erinstumpprojects.com

Bright little art gallery in the Dundas West neighborhood that features mostly the work of up-and-coming artists from the Toronto area.

D4 ✉ 1450 Dundas Street West
☎ 647/345-6163 ⏰ Wed–Sat 11–6 🚋 505 Dundas streetcar

FREDA'S

fredas.com

Canadian designer Freda Iordanous dresses a number of TV personalities and actresses, and all her casual, business and evening garments for women are produced on the premises. Lines from Europe are also stocked.

G7 ✉ 86 Bathurst Street ☎ 416/703-0304 or 1-888/373-3271 ⏰ Mon–Wed and Sat 9.30–6, Thu 9.30–8 🚋 511 Bathurst or 504 King streetcars

FRESH COLLECTIVE

freshcollective.com

Kensington Market clothing and accessory store with an original flair featuring local designers and unique international labels.

H5 ✉ 274 Augusta Avenue ☎ 416/966-0123 ⏰ Mon–Sat 11–7, Sun 12–6 🚋 505 Dundas streetcar

GOTSTYLE

gotstyle.com

The place in the Fashion District for modern menswear, with designer brands, independent labels, accessories and shoes. There's a vintage barber shop too.

➕ G7 ✉ 62 Bathurst Street ☎ 416/260-9696 🕐 Mon–Fri 11–8, Sat 11–6, Sun 12–5 🚃 504 King or 511 Bathurst streetcars

JOHN FLUEVOG

fluevog.com

The most flamboyant shoes imaginable are found at this stylish outlet. Madonna and Lady Gaga have both been known to shop in this store.

➕ K6 ✉ 686 Queen Street West ☎ 416/581-1420 🕐 Mon–Wed 11–7, Thu–Sat 10–8, Sun 11–6 🚇 Osgoode 🚃 501 Queen streetcar

LAVISH & SQUALOR

lavishandsqualor.com

This is an independent hipster haven with unique clothing labels, accessories, handmade crafts and homeware for sale, plus there's the bonus of an espresso bar and art gallery.

➕ K6 ✉ 253 Queen Street West ☎ 416/530-0003 🕐 Daily 11–8 🚃 501 Queen streetcar

MOUNTAIN EQUIPMENT CO-OP (MEC)

mec.ca

Even if you're not a climber, you'll find a great range of outdoor clothing, footwear and camping gear here. The store's roof is a sustainable re-creation of a prairie environment and the store takes in old batteries for recycling.

➕ J7 ✉ 400 King Street West ☎ 416/340-2667 🕐 Mon–Sat 9–9, Sun 9–6 🚃 504 King Street West or 510 Spadina streetcars

SONIC BOOM

sonicboommusic.com

The definitive place for vinyl, both new and used. Find a large collection of CDs, Blu-ray and DVDs and even old cassette tapes here, with a selection of T-shirts and turntables too.

➕ G2 ✉ 215 Spadina Avenue ☎ 416/532-0334 🕐 Daily 10–10 🚃 511 Bathurst streetcar

TEN REN'S TEA

tenrenstea.com

In the heart of Chinatown, this store stocks an excellent range of fine teas in urns and also sells health-oriented infusions and slimming tea. You will also find a superb stock of tiny Chinese teapots and teacups in a range of patterns and colors.

➕ J5 ✉ 454 Dundas Street West at Huron ☎ 416/598-7872 🚃 505 Dundas streetcar

TORONTO ANTIQUES ON KING

High-quality antiques dealers, well known in their specialties, operate the dozen booths here. Shoppers will find estate jewelry, maps and prints, porcelain, silver, Oriental rugs, scientific instruments and much more.

➕ K7 ✉ 284 King Street West at Duncan ☎ 416/260-9057 🚇 St. Andrew

BOOKSTORES GALORE

Toronto's independent booksellers continue to thrive once again. Local independents include the elegant **Ben McNally Books** (▷ 57), offering fewer mainstream choices, **The Beguiling Books & Art** (➕ G2 ✉ 319 College Street ☎ 416/533-9168, beguilingbooksandart.com) and **Book City**, with four stores: Yonge Street, Danforth Avenue, Queen Street East and Bloor Street West.

Entertainment and Nightlife

BARHOP

barhopbar.com

A fantastic bar serving 36 craft beers on tap and over 100 bottled and canned varieties. The good modern menu focuses on comfort foods. Enjoy people watching from the street-side patio.

J7 ✉ 91 King Street West ☎ 647/352-7476 🚋 504 King streetcar

EL CONVENTO RICO

elconventorico.com

Famed for its weekend 1am drag shows, this basement club draws a LGBTQ and straight crowd of all ages. Lambada the night away until 4am.

F3 ✉ 750 College Street at Crawford ☎ 416/588-7800 🚋 506 Carlton streetcar

CROCODILE ROCK

crocrock.ca

Bar-restaurant and dance space with a pool lounge. Music is mostly Top 40, plus some retro tunes.

K6 ✉ 240 Adelaide Street West at Duncan ☎ 416/599-9751 🚇 St. Andrew

DRAKE HOTEL BAR

thedrakehotel.ca

In an artsy hotel, there's an eclectic program of live music and DJs. Offerings include soul, funk, reggae, jazz, opera and French *chanson*.

D6 ✉ 1150 Queen Street West ☎ 416/531-5042 🚋 501 Queen streetcar

THE ELGIN AND WINTER GARDEN THEATRE CENTRE

heritagetrust.on.ca

Owned and run by the Ontario Heritage Trust, these last surviving Edwardian stacked theatres perform shows that are opulent and highly memorable.

M6 ✉ 189 Yonge Street ☎ 416/314-2901 🚇 Queen

FACTORY THEATRE

factorytheatre.ca

This theater is dedicated to producing the works of new Canadian playwrights, which are put on in two theaters.

H6 ✉ 125 Bathurst ☎ 416/504-9971 🚋 511 Bathurst streetcar

THE FIFTH

thefifth.com

The crowd here (and sometimes visiting celebrities) gathers in the loft-like space. The music leans to lounge and allows for conversation.

K6 ✉ 221 Richmond Street West ☎ 416/979-0390 🚇 Osgoode

HORSESHOE TAVERN

horseshoetavern.com

Established in 1947, this is where The Police, The Band, Blue Rodeo and Barenaked Ladies launched in Canada.

J6 ✉ 370 Queen Street West ☎ 416/598-4226 🚋 501 Queen streetcar

NORTHWOOD

northwoodto.ca

Café by day, bar by night, this Victorian/industrial-designed space focuses on local craft breweries, Ontario wines and a Canadian-inspired liquor selection.

F2 ✉ 815 Bloor Street West ☎ 416/846-8324 🚇 Ossington

TICKETS & INFORMATION

Get tickets, including day-of-performance half-price admission, at the TO Tix booth at Yonge-Dundas Square (➕ M5 🚇 Tue–Sat 12–6 ☎ 416/645-9090 or 888/655-9090, totix.ca). To find out what's on, try *Toronto Life*, *Where Toronto* and the weekend editions of the *Globe & Mail*, *Toronto Star* and *Toronto Sun*. *Now* covers the latest trends, and *Xtra!* LGBTQ scene in the city.

ORBIT ROOM

orbitroom.ca

Co-founded by Alex Lifeson of Canada's legendary rock band Rush, this continues to be a premier venue for live R&B, funk, alternative rock and jazz.

🔲 G4 ✉ 580A College Street ☎ 416/535-0613 🚋 506 Carlton streetcar

PRINCESS OF WALES THEATRE

mirvish.com

This 2,000-seat theater has one of the largest stages in North America and clever three-level seating gives excellent sight-lines. The acoustics are nearly perfect and the craftsmanship is superb—the murals alone are worth a visit.

🔲 K7 ✉ 300 King Street West at John Street ☎ 416/872-1212, 1-800/461-3333 tickets 🚋 504 King streetcar

REX HOTEL JAZZ AND BLUES BAR

therex.ca

This club offers top local and up-and-coming modern jazz artists and a great night out.

🔲 K6 ✉ 194 Queen Street West ☎ 416/598-2475 🚋 501 Queen streetcar

ROYAL ALEXANDRA THEATRE

mirvish.com

The century-old theater has been played by many of the all-time greats of the stage, including John Gielgud, Orson Welles, Fred Astaire, and the Marx Brothers. The interior remains the epitome of a 19th-century theater.

🔲 K7 ✉ 260 King Street West at Duncan ☎ 416/872-1212, 1-800/461-3333 tickets, 416/593-0351 admin 🚋 504 King streetcar

ROY THOMSON HALL

roythomson.com

This is the foremost concert hall in Canada. It's the home of Toronto Symphony Orchestra, and the greatest international orchestras and classical performers also play here, with occasional world culture and other genres. Check the website for details of forthcoming events and performances.

🔲 K7 ✉ 60 Simcoe Street ☎ 416/872-4255 box office 🚋 504 King streetcar

SECOND CITY

secondcity.com

This venue is the source of many well-known Canadian comedians who have made it big internationally—Mike Myers, John Candy, Dan Aykroyd, Bill Murray, Martin Short, and others, so it's the place to spot new talent.

🔲 J7 ✉ 51 Mercer Street ☎ 416/343-0011 🚋 504 King streetcar

THEATRE PASSE MURAILLE

passemuraille.ca

This is another theater company that nurtures contemporary Canadian playwrights. It produces an excellent program of innovative and provocative works by such figures as Daniel David Moses and Wajdi Mouawad. There are two stages, one catering to an audience of 185, the other for just 55.

🔲 H6 ✉ 16 Ryerson Avenue ☎ 416/504-7529 🚋 501 Queen streetcar

CLASSICAL COMPANIES

Two Toronto institutions perform principally at Roy Thomson Hall. The Toronto Symphony is the city's premier orchestra. In addition to its classical repertoire, it plays light popular music and its outdoor summer concerts are well supported. The Toronto Mendelssohn Choir performs great choral works, and is noted for Handel's *Messiah*. The choir performed on the soundtrack of the movie *Schindler's List*.

Where to Eat

PRICES

Prices are approximate, based on a
3-course meal for one person.

$$$$	over $80
$$$	$60–$80
$$	$35–$60
$	under $35

360 AT THE CN TOWER ($$$$)

cntower.ca

Don't write this revolving restaurant off
as a tourist trap. It is a fine-dining experience, with an extensive à la carte menu
of impressive dishes, including prime
beef, Atlantic salmon and lobster, and
Ontario pickerel.

K8 ⊠ 301 Front Street West ☎ 416/362-
5411 ⊙ From 11am daily ⊜ Union

BORALIA ($)

boraliato.com

You'll dine on top-quality Canadian
ingredients here. Some of the expertly
crafted traditional recipes date back to
pioneer times (look for dates of origin
on the menu). Try pemmican salad with
cured bison and wild rice, a hearty
Acadian chicken fricot, or roast venison.
Bring someone with similar tastes,
though as main courses are for sharing.

E5 ⊠ 59 Ossington Avenue ☎ 647/351-
5100 ⊙ Wed–Sun from 5.30pm ⊜ 01
Queen or 63 Ossington streetcar

CAFÉ DIPLOMATICO ($)

cafediplomatico.ca

Still resisting gentrification, Diplomatico
has mosaic marble floors, wrought-iron
chairs and a glorious cappuccino
machine. A Toronto tradition on
weekends.

G4 ⊠ 594 College Street ☎ 416/534-
4637 ⊙ Sun–Thu 8am–1am, Fri, Sat 8am–2am
⊜ 506 Carlton streetcar

CHIADO ($$$$)

chiadorestaurant.com

Sophisticated and elegant, this spacious
restaurant has art on the walls and pro-
gressive Portuguese cuisine on the plate.
Signature dishes are marinated sardines,
poached salted cod and *natas do céu*.

E3 ⊠ 864 College Street, at Concord
Avenue ☎ 416/538-1910 ⊙ Mon–Fri
12–2.30 and 5–10, Sat–Sun 5–10 ⊜ 506
Carlton streetcar

DEATH IN VENICE ($)

deathinvenice.ca

Good for hearty breakfasts, quick
lunches and refreshing ice creams.
Vegan options extend to the gelato, and
there's a huge range of unusual and
downright adventurous flavors.

H6 ⊠ 536 Queen Street West
☎ 416/519-3451 ⊙ Mon–Thu 9–9, Fri 9am–
10pm, Sat 10–10, Sun 10–9 ⊜ 501 Queen
streetcar

DUMPLING HOUSE RESTAURANT ($)

It's in the middle of Chinatown—fast service and cheap prices. Watch the cooks
roll the dough and fill it with pork and
chives—their most popular dumpling.

J5 ⊠ 328 Spadina Avenue ☎ 416/596-
8898 ⊙ Wed–Mon 11am–11pm ⊜ 505
Dundas streetcar

A FEW TIPS

Restaurant checks (bills) include a 13 percent harmonized sales tax (HST), though
prepared food and beverages under $4 are
tax-exempt. Always tip on the pretax total
of the check. All restaurants are smoke-
free. Well-dressed casual is acceptable in
most restaurants. Men might feel more
comfortable wearing a jacket in the more
upscale dining spots.

EMA-TEI ($$)

ematei.ca

Frequented by many Japanese visitors because of its authentic cuisine, from perfect appetizers to fresh sushi.

➕ K6 ✉ 30 St. Patrick Street ☎ 416/340-0472 🕐 Tue–Fri 11.45–2.30 and 5.30–9.45, Sat–Sun 5.30–9.45 🚇 Osgoode

FRED'S NOT HERE ($$)

fredsnothere.com

A huge, glowing mural and open kitchen share the limelight with a long, eclectic menu with Mediterranean and Oriental influences alongside comfort food.

➕ K6 ✉ 321 King Street West ☎ 416/971-9155 🕐 Wed–Sun lunch from 11.30, dinner from 4.30, Mon–Tue dinner from 4.30 🚋 504 King streetcar

FUSARO'S ITALIAN KITCHEN ($$)

fusaros.com

Authentic southern Italian eatery with lunch queues out the door. Try the delcious paninis for under $10.

➕ J6 ✉ 147 Spadina Avenue ☎ 416/260-8414 🕐 Mon–Fri 9–9, Sat 11–6. Closed Sun 🚋 501 Queen streetcar

MATAHARI ($)

mataharigrill.com

Chic and modern, this bar and grill offers a fusion of Asian and Indian cuisines in colorful dishes with sauces spiced with lime leaf, chilis and red onion, spring rolls and satays, served in a halogen-lit setting or out on the patio.

➕ J4 ✉ 39 Baldwin Street (off Spadina) ☎ 416/596-2832 🕐 Mon–Fri 11.30–9.30, Sat 4.30–10 🚇 St. Patrick

LE SÉLECT BISTRO ($–$$)

leselect.com

Select is as French as they come, from the *pied-de-cochon* to the background jazz. The weekend brunch is popular so it's worth making a reservation.

➕ H7 ✉ 432 Wellington Street West ☎ 416/596-6405 🕐 Mon–Wed 11.30–11, Thu–Fri 11.30–11.30, Sat 11am–midnight, Sun 10.30–10.30 🚋 504 King streetcar

QUEEN MOTHER CAFÉ ($$)

queenmothercafe.ca

A friendly and characterful highlight of Queen Street West, its eclectic menu is strong on Asian classics. There's a secluded, sheltered patio out back.

➕ K6 ✉ 208 Queen Street West ☎ 416/598-4719 🕐 Mon–Wed 11.30am–midnight; Thu–Sat 11.30am–1am, Sun 11.30am–11pm 🚋 501 Queen streetcar

STELVIO ($$–$$$)

stelviotoronto.ca

With another branch in Milan, Stelvio offers truly authentic cuisine. The pasta and gnocchi is all house-made.

➕ J6 ✉ 354 Queen Street West ☎ 416/205-1001 🕐 Tue–Thu 5–10pm, Fri–Sun 11–3 and 5–11 🚋 501 Queen streetcar

WAH SING ($$)

wahsing.ca

A seafood hotspot for deep-fried oysters, Peking duck and, in season, two lobsters for the price of one.

➕ K4 ✉ 47 Baldwin Street ☎ 416/599-8822 🕐 Daily 11.30–11 🚋 505 Dundas streetcar

---

TABLES WITH A VIEW

On the 54th floor of the TD Bank Tower, **Canoe** offers skyscrapers views. On top of the Park Hyatt, the **Roof Lounge** (✉ 4 Avenue Road) has great downtown views. **Scaramouche** (✉ 1 Benvenuto Place ☎ 416/961-8011) has window seats over the downtown skyline. The best view is from **360** on top of the CN Tower (▷ 39).

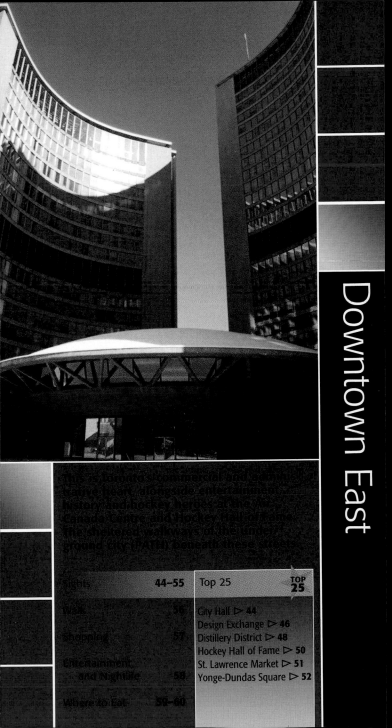

Downtown East

This is Toronto's commercial and political (native heart, alongside entertainment, history and hockey heroes at the Air Canada Centre and Hockey Hall of Fame. The sheltered walkways of the underground city (PATH) beneath these streets.

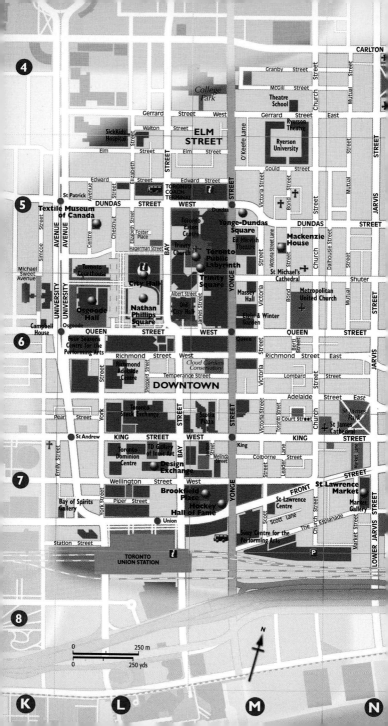

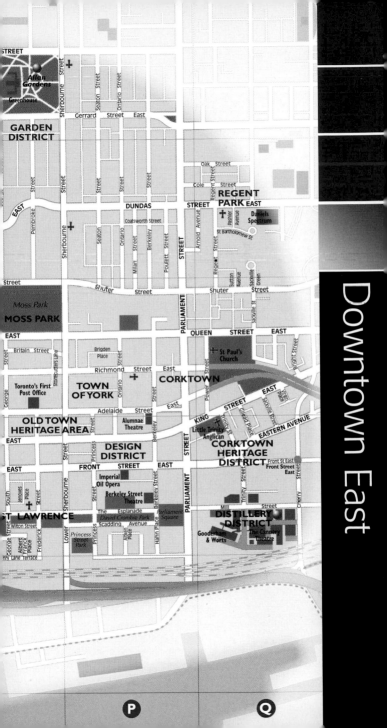

STREET

Allan Gardens
Greenhouse

GARDEN DISTRICT

Sherbourne Street
Seaton Street
Ontario Street
Gerrard Street East

Pembroke Street

EAST

Sherbourne

Seaton

Ontario

Berkeley Street

Poulett Street

DUNDAS

Oak Street

Cole Street

REGENT PARK EAST

Daniels Spectrum

Parliament Avenue

Regent Street

St Bartholomew St.

Coatsworth Street

Milan

STREET

Arnold Avenue

Sutton Avenue

Sackville Green

Sackville St

Street

Ghuter Street

Shuter Street

PARLIAMENT

Moss Park

MOSS PARK

EAST

QUEEN STREET EAST

Britain Street

Stonecutters Lane

Street

Brigden Place

Richmond Street East

Ontario Street

CORKTOWN

St Paul's Church

Eight Street

Toronto's First Post Office

George

TOWN OF YORK

Power Street

EAST

STREET

Sackville Street

Adelaide Street East

OLD TOWN HERITAGE AREA

Alumnae Theatre

Berkeley Street

KING

Cherry Street

EASTERN AVENUE

EAST

Princess Street

DESIGN DISTRICT

STREET

Gilead Place

Little Trinity Anglican

CORKTOWN HERITAGE DISTRICT

Front St East
Front Street East

EAST

FRONT STREET EAST

Sherbourne Street

Imperial Oil Opera

Berkeley Street Theatre

PARLIAMENT

Trinity Street

ST LAWRENCE

South Jenoves Place

Lower

The Esplanade
David Crombie Park
Scadding Avenue

Princess Street Park

Aitken Place

Hahn Place

Parliament Square

Mill Street

DISTILLERY DISTRICT

Gooderham & Worts

The Cannery Theatre

Cherry Street

Wilton Street

George Street

Albert Franck Place

Frederick

nny Lane Terrace

P   **Q**

City Hall

- Council Chamber
- Hall of Memory
- *Metropolis*
- Henry Moore's *Three Way Piece No. 2* ("The Archer")
- Podium Green Roof

TIP

- Guided tours are only available to groups, but the website has a good down-loadable self-guiding tour.

Remarkable for its striking design, which shook up Toronto in the early 1960s, City Hall could be a space station, with the council chamber a flying saucer cradled between two semicircular control towers.

Viljo Revell and Nathan Phillips When Mayor Nathan Phillips persuaded the City Council to hold a competition to design a new city hall, the councillors received 520 submissions from 42 countries. Finnish architect Viljo Revell won, and his building opened in 1965. The square in front is a site for entertainment; the reflecting pool, where workers eat sandwiches in summer, is a skating rink in winter. To the east of City Hall, the Peace Garden contains an eternal flame lit by Pope John Paul II using a flame from the Memorial for Peace at Hiroshima.

Clockwise from left: City Hall with the old town hall clock tower; nighttime view from above; City Hall's curving lobby; Henry Moore's sculpture "The Archer"; daytime view of City Hall from below

Near the entrance stands Henry Moore's *Three Way Piece No. 2*, affectionately called "The Archer" by Torontonians.

Municipal art City Hall itself contains several artworks. Just inside the entrance, the mural *Metropolis*, by local artist David Partridge, is created from more than 100,000 nails. Continue into the Rotunda and the Hall of Memory, shaped like a sunken amphitheater, where, in the Golden Book of Remembrance, are listed 3,500 Torontonians who died in World War II. At its center rises a white column supporting the Council Chamber above. The north corridor is lined with a copper-and-glass mosaic called *Views to the City*, depicting historic panoramas of the skyline. From here you can take an elevator to the Council Chamber.

THE BASICS

toronto.ca

✚ L6

✉ 100 Queen Street West

☎ 416/338-0338

🕐 Mon–Fri 8.30–4.30

🍴 Caféteria

Ⓠ Queen or Osgoode

♿ Very good

💲 Free

❓ Self-guided tour

Design Exchange

HIGHLIGHTS

● The frieze on the facade
● Murals by Charles Comfort
● The staircase
● Canadian Industrial Design collection

TIPS

● Try to attend one of the Mastercraft Workshops with a top designer.
● The gift shop, not surprisingly, has better-designed goods than most.

Housed in the former Stock Exchange, the Design Exchange was established in the 1980s to promote Canadian design and to encourage more appreciation of the applied arts.

The building In 1986 the city council was persuaded that a design center would be a good idea, but it wasn't until 1994 that it held its official opening in the fine heritage building recently vacated by the Toronto Stock Exchange. Now encased by the TD Centre, the pink granite and limestone facade stands out against the surrounding black-and-glass structure—a frame that serves to emphasize the symmetry of the early 20th-century design. Inside is equally impressive, with some remarkable murals and a fine staircase.

Clockwise from left: the exterior of the building; northeast view of the trading floor of the old Stock Exchange; staircase of the trading floor; murals

The exhibits No other museum in Canada has a collection that is so focused on the preservation of the nation's modern industrial design. The permanent collection includes more than 600 items of furniture, industrial design, homewares, textiles, lighting and other themes, although not all can be on show. It's fun to look back over 70 years of chair design and to see the first item acquired by the Design Exchange—the stylish but bulky Project G2 Stereo. The DX stages exhibitions every year to highlight aspects of design, in the Chalmers Design Centre and Teknion Lounge at ground level and in the 3rd-floor Exhibition Hall. Recent exhibitions have included themes on digital fabrication in interior design and 1990s design. A highlight of the year is the Design Exchange Awards.

THE BASICS

dx.org

✚ L7

✉ 234 Bay Street

☎ 416/363-6121

🕐 Tue–Fri 9–5, Sat–Sun noon–4.30

🍴 Restaurants, café and food hall in TD Centre

Ⓚ King or Union

🚋 504 King streetcar

♿ Very good

✋ Free

❓ Tours last Fri of month noon–1

Distillery District

HIGHLIGHTS

● Wandering the
cobbled streets
● Distillery walking tour
and Segway tours
● Glass artists at work in
the Tank studio
● Thompson Landry
Gallery
● Corkin Gallery
● Mill Street Brewery tour

TIP

● Movie, TV and music
video filming might
occasionally block off some
areas. On the plus side,
you might spot some
famous actors and singers
at work.

**Vibrant, artsy and atmospheric, this is not
only a great place to shop for artisan
crafts and original art but it's also a venue
for live music and festivals. It's a far cry
from the rundown former distillery that
used to occupy these buildings.**

Where it began William Gooderham's and
James Worts' waterfront distillery started up in
1837, and soon became the world's largest
distillery. In 1987, this now-disused but outstanding example of Victorian industrial design
was acquired by Allied Lyons, which spent $25
million on its preservation.

Everything old is new Eventually, visionary
developers purchased the 13-acre (5ha) site
and installed new life. Original concrete floors,

Clockwise from left: Balzacs Coffee Roasters; a restored warehouse; heart sculpture on Gristmill Lane; an aerial view of Trinity Street; El Catrin Mexican restaurant on Tank House Lane

brick walls and beamed ceilings are unchanged. More than 340,000 old bricks were laid in the lanes, and now creative tenants add to the atmosphere. The district's original purpose has also been revived by two craft distilleries.

Arts and culture About 30 festivals take place each year. Original distillery buildings now house a microbrewery making organic beer, art galleries, nearly 20 artists' studios and lots of interesting stores and boutiques. Goods range from clothing and jewelry to furniture. The performing arts have a large presence, including theater and dance companies and performance schools. The Young Centre for the Performing Arts, with partners George Brown College and Soulpepper Theatre, occupy a complex that includes four performing spaces.

THE BASICS

thedistillerydistrict.com

✚ Q7

✉ Between Mill Street, Parliament Street and Cherry Street

☎ 416/364-1177

🕐 Site 10am; stores and galleries, hours vary

🍴 Many outlets

🚇 Union then 121 bus to Mill and Cherry Street

🚃 514 Cherry streetcar to Cherry Street or 504 King streetcar to Parliament Street

♿ Good

💷 Free; tours moderate

❓ Various tours

Hockey Hall of Fame

Exhibits (left); replica of the Stanley Cup (right)

THE BASICS

hhof.com

✚ M7

✉ Brookfield Place at 30 Yonge Street

☎ 416/360-7765

🕐 Late Jun–early Sep and Mar break Mon–Sat 9.30–6, Sun 10–6; Sep–May Mon–Fri 10–5, Sat 9.30–6, Sun 10.30–5

🚇 King or Union Station

🚋 504 King streetcar

♿ Very good

💰 Moderate

HIGHLIGHTS

● Stanley Cup
● NHLPA Game Time
● Montréal Canadiens' dressing room
● Shootout Zone
● The 3D *Stanley's Game Seven* film

There's a Canadian saying: First you walk, then you skate. It would not be an exaggeration to say that practically the entire nation is fanatical about the game, and this is its temple of excellence.

The Stanley Cup and Hall of Fame The jewel of the museum is the Esso Great Hall, once the grand banking hall of the Bank of Montreal. Here the Stanley Cup, North America's oldest professional sports trophy, is displayed in front of the Honoured Members Wall.

Live action At the NHLPA Game Time you can shoot on a model rink, with real sticks and pucks; or you can play goalkeeper against some of hockey's greatest players in the interactive Shut Out game, which even comes with a recording of your performance you can share on social media.

A hockey tour From the entrance lobby, you pass into the NHL Zone, with multimedia displays and memorabilia about all aspects of the NHL and its milestone moments and teams. From there it's a journey through the world of hockey, including an interactive Broadcast Zone, simulators, theaters showing hockey events, displays of artifacts and trophies, a re-creation of the Montréal Canadiens' locker room, places to pick up some memorabilia of your own, and more. Before you leave check out the fun Our Game bronze and Team Canada '72 monument outside the building.

TOP 25

St. Lawrence Market

The lofty 19th-century building that houses this market is entirely worthy of the rich displays within. This is the place to taste a Canadian peameal bacon sandwich or buy the ingredients for a picnic.

Food-lovers' favorites There are more than 120 vendors in the market, all of them experts in their own specialty, and the array of cheeses, meats, vegetables, deli goods, seafood, baked goods and gourmet treats is irresistible. There's a great atmosphere when the market is crowded with happy shoppers, delighting in new discoveries, confidently heading for their favorite vendors, or offering helpful hints to out-of-towners. Vendors will often offer tastings and, when it's not so busy, take the time to chat about their products. In addition to the foods, a few artisans have stands here, including clothing, jewelry and Toronto souvenirs.

Get involved It's worth checking out the events at the market, which might include a cookery class, a themed supper club or one of the popular talks that's often accompanied by an English-style afternoon tea.

Fresh from the fields On Saturday farmers set up stalls at daybreak in the farmers' market building across the street, selling fresh produce, preserves, fresh baking, meat, and arts and crafts. On Sunday, the wares are a little different, when around 80 antique dealers fill the North Market Hall.

THE BASICS

stlawrencemarket.com

➕ N7

🏢 92 Front Street East

☎ 416/392-7219

🕐 Tue–Thu 8–6, Fri 8–7, Sat 5–5; farmers' market Sat 5–5

🚇 King or Union

🚃 504 King streetcar

♿ Good

🎟 Free

HIGHLIGHTS

- Sausage King
- Carousel Bakery
- Carnicero's
- Future Bakery
- Scheffler's Deli
- Alex Farm Products
- Caviar Direct

Yonge–Dundas Square

HIGHLIGHTS

● Free entertainment
● The fountains
● People-watching
● Proximity to shops and nightlife

TIPS

● Bring dry clothes for your kids. Those fountains are irresistible on a warm day (water is filtered and solar-heated, and play is encouraged).
● As in any crowded city spot, watch out for pickpockets.

New York has Times Square, London has Piccadilly Circus, and Toronto has Yonge-Dundas Square as its downtown hub, open-air entertainment venue, and the place to go just to feel that city vibe.

At the once-traffic-clogged intersection of the city's busiest streets, the square was created soon after the millennium to provide a focal point. Colorful hoardings, several stories high, and digital displays draw the eye to the surrounding buildings, while 22 fountains jet up from the ground (weather permitting). Sidewalk cafés revive weary shoppers, buskers perform and the people-watching is superlative.

The square experience It's clean and compact, and you're likely to find something going

Clockwise from left: the bright lights of Yonge-Dundas Square; the popular Toronto Pride parade; flagship stores flank the square

on. As well as street entertainers, there are organized diversions, including free concerts and movie screenings. Wander to the corner of Dundas and look through the window of the City TV studio to see who's on. There's also a ticket booth for shows at city venues.

Festival fun Hundreds of festivals, concerts and community events take over the square during the year. It's a great place to see in the New Year or to watch the Christmas tree lighting ceremony in late November. The warmer months bring events such as Ribfest in mid-May, Toronto Pride and the Toronto Jazz Festival in June, Canada Day celebrations on July 1, the Pan American Food and Music Festival and Indonesian Street Festival, both in August, and Toronto International Film Festival in September.

THE BASICS
ydsquare.ca
✚ M5
✉ 1 Dundas Street
🕐 Always open
Ⓡ Yonge or Dundas
♿ Good
💲 Free

More to See

ALLAN GARDENS

Just a short way east of busy Yonge Street, this peaceful haven is a horticultural gem. It has six greenhouses, the best being the glass-domed Palm House, which was modeled on the one at London's Kew Gardens.

➕ N4 ✉ 19 Horticultural Avenue, off Gerrard Street ☎ 416/392-7288 🕐 Daily 10–5 🚇 College 🚹 Good ⚡ Free

BROOKFIELD PLACE

The highlight of this Financial District commerce and retail complex is the stunning Allen Lambert Galleria, a glittering six-story high atrium of curved steel and glass, designed by Santiago Calatrava. It's worth a special journey just to walk through it. Brookfield Place contains a select range of interesting stores like Crème de la Crème lingerie, designer menswear at Pace, and avant-garde footwear at Stepss, plus places to refuel.

➕ M7 ✉ 181 Bay Street ☎ 416/777-6480 🕐 Daily 7.30–5.45 🚇 Union 🚹 Good

MACKENZIE HOUSE

Toronto's first mayor, William Lyon Mackenzie, lived here from 1859 until his death in 1861 and it now acts as a museum of his life. An outspoken journalist, he published the *Colonial Advocate*, and the house has a re-creation of his printshop. Other displays recall his turbulent political life, including the failed Upper Canada Rebellion.

➕ M5 ✉ 82 Bond Street ☎ 416/392-6915 🕐 May–early Sep Tue–Sun 12–5; Sep–Dec Tue–Fri 12–4, Sat–Sun 12–5; Jan–Apr Sat–Sun 12–5 (Mar break Mon–Fri 12–4, Sat–Sun 12–5 🚇 Dundas 🚹 Few ⚡ Inexpensive

NATHAN PHILLIPS SQUARE

Overlooked by the incredible City Hall building, this is a major meeting place, where office workers bring their lunch in the summer, and tourists flock to view the Henry Moore sculpture, the fountain and the Peace Garden's reflecting pool and eternal flame. Concerts and other events take place here throughout spring and summer,

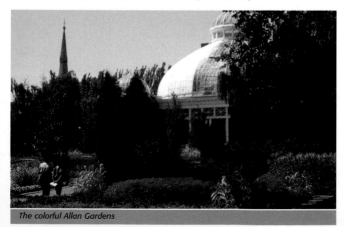

The colorful Allan Gardens

and in winter skaters glide on the huge rink.

⊞ L6 ⊠ 100 Queen Street West ⊚ Queen or Osgoode

OSGOODE HALL

osgoodehall.com and and lsuc.on.ca/visit
This building (1829) houses the headquarters of Ontario's legal profession, with an elegant interior and an impressive portrait and sculpture collection. There are many rooms to see, by self-guided audio tour or guided by a staff member, including the stunning Great Library and American Room, the courtrooms (guided tour only), and Convocation Hall, with its superb stained-glass windows. Throughout, there are outstanding tiled floors and other architectural features. The building is set on lawns and flower beds. While there, try the Osgoode Hall Restaurant for lunch (▷ 60).

⊞ L6 ⊠ 130 Queen Street West
☎ 416/947-3300 ⊚ Mon–Fri 9–5 for self-guided audio tours; guided tours daily at 1.15 July–Aug (except first Mon in Aug) ⊚ Osgoode ⊛ Few ⊕ Free

TEXTILE MUSEUM OF CANADA

textilemuseum.ca
This gem of a museum has a huge permanent collection of 12,000 textiles, some as old as 2,000 years, from all over the world. Items on show change regularly, with themed exhibitions such as Latin American weaving and dying techniques, Victorian needlework, or Japanese textiles and garments.

⊞ L5 ⊠ 55 Centre Avenue ☎ 416/599-5321 ⊚ Daily 11–5 (Wed to 8)
⊚ St. Patrick ⊛ Very good ⊕ Moderate

TRINITY SQUARE AND TORONTO PUBLIC LABYRINTH

The Church of the Holy Trinity sits in a little park just west of the CF Toronto Eaton Centre. Built in 1847, the church now overlooks a labyrinth, some 23m (77ft) across. The theory is that by walking in these ever-decreasing circles you will center yourself and thus aid creative thinking or gain a problem-solving mind-set. It's worth a try.

⊞ M5 ⊚ Dundas

A splendid hat (above) and a silk kimono (right) on display at the Textile Museum of Canada

Historic Highlights

Explore some of Toronto's oldest areas, including the Distillery Historic District and one of the best food markets in Canada.

DISTANCE: 3km (1.8 miles) **ALLOW:** 3 hours

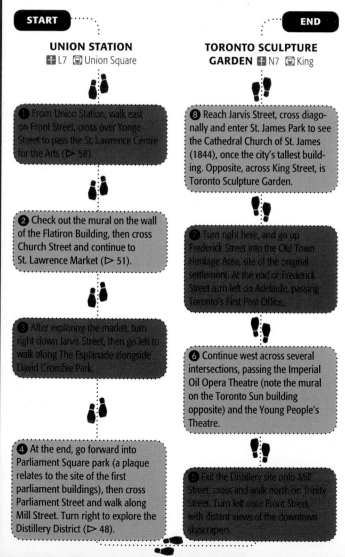

START

UNION STATION
✚ L7 🔲 Union Square

❶ From Union Station, walk east on Front Street, cross over Yonge Street to pass the St. Lawrence Centre for the Arts (▷ 58).

❷ Check out the mural on the wall of the Flatiron Building, then cross Church Street and continue to St. Lawrence Market (▷ 51).

❸ After exploring the market, turn right down Jarvis Street, then go left to walk along The Esplanade alongside David Crombie Park.

❹ At the end, go forward into Parliament Square park (a plaque relates to the site of the first parliament buildings), then cross Parliament Street and walk along Mill Street. Turn right to explore the Distillery District (▷ 48).

END

TORONTO SCULPTURE GARDEN ✚ N7 🔲 King

❽ Reach Jarvis Street, cross diagonally and enter St. James Park to see the Cathedral Church of St. James (1844), once the city's tallest building. Opposite, across King Street, is Toronto Sculpture Garden.

❼ Turn right here, and go up Frederick Street into the Old Town Heritage Area, site of the original settlement. At the end of Frederick Street turn left on Adelaide, passing Toronto's First Post Office.

❻ Continue west across several intersections, passing the Imperial Oil Opera Theatre (note the mural on the Toronto Sun building opposite) and the Young People's Theatre.

❺ Exit the Distillery site onto Mill Street, cross and walk north on Trinity Street. Turn left onto Front Street, with distant views of the downtown skyscrapers.

8TH AND MAIN

8main.ca

The Toronto outpost of this British Columbia-based chain has up-to-the-minute casual clothing for men and women at reasonable prices.

➕ M6 ✉ 211 Yonge Street ☎ 647/348-1222 ◷ Mon–Wed 10–8, Thu–Sat 10–9, Sun 10–7 🚇 Queen

BAY OF SPIRITS GALLERY

bayofspirits.com

Sells a wide range of First Nations artwork including Ojibwe, Iroquois, Inuit, and Haida art.

➕ L7 ✉ 156 Front Street West ☎ 416/971-5190 ◷ Mon–Sat 10–6 🚇 Union

BEN MCNALLY BOOKS

benmcnallybooks.com

This excellent independent bookseller has a loyal following and a warm, wood-paneled space like an old library.

➕ L6 ✉ 366 Bay Street ☎ 416/361-0032 ◷ Mon–Fri 9–6, Sat 11–5 (except holiday weekends) 🚋 501 Queen streetcar

BERGO DESIGNS

bergodesigns.ca

Unique industrial design applied to a mind-boggling range of goods and gifts. Some eye-popping prices but there's great browsing value.

➕ Q7 ✉ 28 Tank House Lane ☎ 416/861-1821 ◷ Mon–Sat 10–9, Sun 10–7 🚇 Union then 121 bus to Mill Street and Cherry Street 🚋 514 Cherry streetcar

CF TORONTO EATON CENTRE

torontoeatoncentre.com

A million visitors a week shop in this indoor mall on four levels.

➕ M5–M6 ✉ Yonge between Dundas and Queen ☎ 416/598-8560 ◷ Daily 10–9.30 🚇 Dundas or Queen

CORKTOWN DESIGNS

corktowndesigns.com

Unique jewelry from 50+ contemporary Canadian and international artists.

➕ Q7 ✉ 5 Trinity Street ☎ 416/861-3020 ◷ Mon–Thu 10–7, Fri–Sat 10–8, Sun 11–7 🚋 504 King streetcar

HAVEN

havenshop.ca

Loft-like men's clothing store in Corktown with Japanese streetwear, sneakers and backpacks.

➕ P6 ✉ 145 Berkeley Street ☎ 647/344-4745 ◷ Mon–Sat 11–7, Sun and holidays 12–5 🚋 501 Queen streetcar

REAL SPORTS APPAREL

shop.realsports.ca

Sport fans can find approved jerseys and headwear for the Maple Leafs, Raptors, Toronto FC, and the Marlies. There's memorabilia, signed jerseys and game-worn Maple Leafs equipment.

➕ L8 ✉ Gate 1, Scotiabank Arena, 40 Bay Street ☎ 416/815-5746 ◷ Mon–Fri 10–7, Sat 10–6, Sun 11–6 (extended hours to ticket-holders on game nights)

CANADA'S OWN

Check out Canadian fashion talent at Hudson's Bay and Holt Renfrew. In the Bloor-Yorkville area you'll find Canada's best-known designers: Vivian Shyu (elegant women's fashion); Linda Lundstrom (casual, but dressy, designs); and Cat's Cradle (classic dresses). Queen Street West is the domain of young designers: John Fluevog (shoes); Caroline Lim at Champagne and Cupcakes (frocks); Kendra Francis at Franke (nightlife outfits); Lowon Pope (sexy, fun and fanciful); Brian Bailey (imaginative urban chic); and Rebecca Nixon at Girl Friday (feminine and timeless).

Entertainment and Nightlife

BERKELEY STREET THEATRE

canadianstage.com

In a converted historic building, the Canadian Stage Company stages varied works, from groundbreaking international works to Shakespeare.

➕ P7 ✉ 26 Berkeley Street ☎ 416/367-8243 🚋 504 King Streetcar

C'EST WHAT

cestwhat.com

A comfortable cellar-style bar for quiet conversation and folk-acoustic music.

➕ M7 ✉ 67 Front Street East ☎ 416/867-9499 🚇 Union

ED MIRVISH THEATRE

mirvish.com

Catch high-profile productions here.

➕ M5 ✉ 244 Victoria Street ☎ 416/872-1212 TicketKing 🚇 Dundas or Queen

ELGIN AND WINTER GARDEN THEATRES

heritagetrust.on.ca

A National Historic Site, this is the only double-decker theater left. If you can't get tickets, take a guided tour.

➕ M6 ✉ 189 Yonge Street ☎ 416/314-2901 🚇 Queen

FOUR SEASONS CENTRE FOR THE PERFORMING ARTS

coc.ca

This magnifient theater is home to the Canadian Opera Company and the National Ballet of Canada.

➕ L6 ✉ 145 Queen Street West ☎ 416/363-6671 🚇 Osgoode

MASSEY HALL

masseyhall.com

This popular live music venue covers genres from classical recitals to blues, jazz and rock bands.

➕ M6 ✉ 178 Victoria Street ☎ 416/872-4255 🚇 Queen

THE RESERVOIR LOUNGE

reservoirlounge.com

This cool spot offers proper martinis, nightly live jazz and decent food.

➕ M7 ✉ 52 Wellington Street East ☎ 416/955-0887 🚋 504 King streetcar

ST. LAWRENCE CENTRE FOR THE ARTS

stlc.com

This focus of Canadian performing arts is dedicated to providing a diverse program of high-quality cultural events.

➕ M7 ✉ 27 Front Street East ☎ 416/366-7723, 1-800/708-6754 box office 🚇 Union

SCOTIABANK ARENA

aircanadacentre.com

Hosts Toronto Maple Leafs hockey team, as well as superstar concerts.

➕ L8 ✉ 40 Bay Street ☎ 416/815-5500 🚇 Union

SONY CENTRE FOR THE PERFORMING ARTS

sonycentre.ca

Big-name concerts, multimedia presentations and short-run shows.

➕ M7 ✉ 1 Front Street East ☎ 1-855/872-7669 🚇 Union

DISTILLERY ARTS

The Distillery District is a cultural center housing the acclaimed Soulpepper Theatre Company, Native Earth Performing Arts, Tapestry Opera, DanceWork, Volcano, Tapestry New Opera Works and the Nightwood Theatre. The complex also includes the superb **Young Centre for the Performing Arts** (✉ 50 Tank House Lane ☎ 416/866-8666).

Where to Eat

ADEGA ($$$)

adegarestaurante.ca

Refined surroundings make this a good special-occasion choice, and you'll want to wear something dressy-casual. Adega gives a contemporary twist to traditional Portuguese dishes, such as a delicious Cataplana fresh fish stew and the Lisbon Tapas Platter. Seafood is the specialty, but there are other choices too, like roasted free-range chicken breast with Duoro red wine jus and garlic mash.
➕ L5 ✉ 33 Elm Street ☎ 416/977-4338
🕐 Mon–Fri 11.30–2 and from 5pm, Sat from 5pm (closing time varies) 🚇 Dundas

BYMARK ($$$$)

bymark.ca

Dramatic decor of wood, glass and water with a delectable menu of classics and service to match. A bar one floor up offers extreme comfort and views. Enjoy the patio in summer.
➕ L7 ✉ 66 Wellington Street West
☎ 416/777-1144 🕐 Mon–Fri 11.30–3 and from 5, Sat from 5 🚇 Union

CANOE ($$$$)

canoerestaurant.com

On the 54th floor of the TDC Bank Tower. Inventive cuisine makes use of Canadian ingredients (West Coast halibut, Alberta lamb, Grandview venison).
➕ L7 ✉ 66 Wellington Street West
☎ 416/364-0054 🕐 Mon–Fri 11.45–2.30 and 5–10.30 🚇 Union

ESPLANADE BIER MARKT ($$)

thebiermarkt.com

A traditional Belgian-themed tile, wood and brick bistro where mussels and French fries are king, with more than 100 bottled beers and others on tap.
➕ P7 ✉ 58 The Esplanade ☎ 416/862-7575
🕐 Sun–Wed 11am–1am, Thu–Sat 11am–2am
🚇 Union

FRAN'S ($)

fransrestaurant.com

A massive menu and 24-hour opening make for a real downtown pleaser. There are a dozen or more breakfast choices, as well as classic comfort food.
➕ M5 ✉ 200 Victoria Street ☎ 416/304-0085 🕐 24 hours 🚇 Queen or Dundas

IRISH EMBASSY PUB & GRILL ($$)

irishembassypub.com

In a splendid old bank building, this place is renowned for its food, from hot breakfasts, through lunchtime sandwiches and bar snacks to entrées.
➕ M7 ✉ 49 Yonge Street ☎ 416/866-8282
🕐 Mon–Fri 11.30am–2am, Sat–Sun 11am–2am
🚇 King

NAMI ($$$)

namirestaurant.ca

Ultrastylish and very expensive, this restaurant serves authentic Japanese cuisine. Prime attractions are the really

fresh sushi and sashimi and darkly
sophisticated interior.

🔹 M6 ✉ 55 Adelaide Street East
☎ 416/362-7373 🕐 Mon–Fri 11.45–2 and
5.30–10, Sat 5.30–10 🚇 Queen or King

OSGOODE HALL RESTAURANT ($)

osgoodehallrestaurant.com

Inside the Court of Appeal for Ontario,
you'll find this fine French lunch spot
filled with judges and old law books.
The food and the service are excellent;
as is the prix-fixe three-course menu.

🔹 L6 ✉ 130 Queen Street West
☎ 416/947-3361 🕐 Mon–Fri 12–2. Closed
Jul–Aug 🚇 501 Queen streetcar

PEARL DIVER ($$)

starfishoysterbed.com

The owner of this comfy and friendly
restaurant is a walking encyclopedia of
seafood lore. The tempting array of oysters, oven-roasted black cod and East
Coast lobsters is just too good to resist.

🔹 N6 ✉ 100 Adelaide Street East
☎ 416/366-7827 🕐 Mon–Fri Mon 4–11, Tue
12–11, Wed 12–12,Thu–Fri 12pm–2am, Sat
11am–2am, Sun 11–11 🚇 King

RUTH'S CHRIS STEAK HOUSE ($$$)

ruthschris.ca

Early dinners and its proximity to a number of entertainment venues make this
an ideal choice for pre-show meals.

🔹 L6 ✉ 145 Richmond Street West
☎ 416/955-1455 or 1-800/544-0808 🕐 Mon–
Thu 5–10, Fri 12–2.30 and 5–10, Sat 4.30–10.30,
Sun 4–9 🚇 Osgoode

SENATOR ($$)

thesenator.com

Claiming to be the city's oldest restaurant, the Senator is in a fine old building
and offers good-value comfort food.

🔹 M5 ✉ 249 Victoria Street ☎ 416/364-
7517 🕐 Mon 7.30am–2.30pm, Tue–Fri
7.30am–9pm, Sat 8–2.30 and 4.30–9, Sun
8–2.30 🚇 Dundas

THE SULTAN'S TENT & CAFÉ MOROC ($$)

thesultanstent.com

With a sumptuously tented interior, this
fine restaurant offers delicious and
beautifully presented Moroccan food,
including tender tagines and flavorsome
couscous dishes. The fixed-price three-
course meals are excellent value, the
service is good and the nightly belly-
dancing shows are a bonus.

🔹 M7 ✉ 49 Front Street East ☎ 416/961-
0601 🕐 Sun–Thu 5–11, Fri 5pm–1am, Sat
12pm–1am 🚇 Union

TUNDRA ($$$)

Well-named for its focus on Canadian
cuisine and wines, even the decor
evokes the barren north. The dinner
menu might include such dishes as
grilled octopus and smoked Haida Gwai
black cod or Dufferin county lamb loin.

🔹 L6 ✉ Hilton Hotel, 145 Richmond Street
West ☎ 416/860-6800 🕐 Mon–Fri 6.30am–
2pm and 5–10, Sat–Sun 7am–2pm and 5–10
🚇 Osgoode

TORONTO EATON CENTRE

Shopping mall eating conjures up fluores-
cent-lit food courts, meals in a bag and
paper cups of coffee, but in the Toronto
Eaton Centre you can do much better. Try
the **City Kitchen**, a casual family-friendly
restaurant with hearty Canadian comfort
foods such as poutine, salmon burgers and
pulled pork sandwiches (✉ Street level
☎ 416/519-5839). Before you rule out
the food court, note it contains **The Urban
Eatery**'s excellent express eats.

Lakeshore and Islands

This is where Toronto relaxes—the south-facing strip alongside Lake Ontario. There are parks, traffic-free paths for walking, cycling and rollerblading, open-air stages and restaurants. The water is busy with kayaks, sailboats and ferries to the islands.

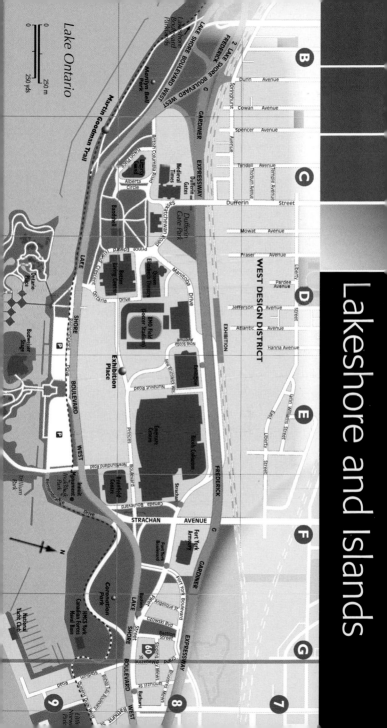

Lakeshore and Islands

Lake Ontario

0 — 250 m
0 — 250 yds

Lake Shore Boulevard Parklands
LAKE SHORE BOULEVARD WEST
FREDERICK
LAKE SHORE BOULEVARD WEST
GARDINER EXPRESSWAY

Martin Goodman Trail

Marilyn Bell Park

British Columbia Road

Medieval Times
Dufferin Gates
Alberta Circle

Bandhell

Saskatchewan Boulevard
Dufferin Gate Park
Princes' Boulevard
Prince Edward Crescent

Betzer Living Centre
Queen Elizabeth Theatre

Ontario Place

Budweiser Stage

LAKE SHORE BOULEVARD WEST

Ontario Drive

Manitoba Drive

BMO Field (Soccer Stadium)

Exhibition Place

Nunavut Road

EXHIBITION

Enercare Centre

Princes' Boulevard

Ricoh Coliseum

FREDERICK

Strachan

Trillium Park

Newfoundland Road
Remembrance Drive

Monument
Inuit Inukshuk Park

Brunfield Centre

Canada Boulevard

STRACHAN AVENUE

Fort York Armoury

Fort York Boulevard

Coronation Park

HMCS York Canadian Forces Naval Base

LAKE SHORE BOULEVARD WEST

GARDINER EXPRESSWAY

Fort York Boulevard

Fleet Street

Angelique St

Czowski Blvd
Bastion Street

National Yacht Club

Little Norway Park

Dan Leckie Way
Queens Quay

LAKE SHORE BOULEVARD WEST

Bathurst

60

Dunn Avenue
Scrimhurst Avenue
Cowan Avenue
Spencer Avenue
Avenue
Tyndall Avenue
Thorburn Avenue
Temple Avenue

Dufferin Street

Mowat Avenue

Fraser Avenue

Liberty Street
Pardee Avenue

WEST DESIGN DISTRICT

Jefferson Avenue

Atlantic Avenue

Hanna Avenue

Lynn Williams Street

East Liberty Street

Liberty Street

B
C
D
E
F
G

9
8
7

Harbourfront Centre

HIGHLIGHTS

● Shopping at Queen's
Quay Terminal
● Art exhibits at the Power
Plant and Bill Boyle Artport
● Craft studio
● Performances
● Free weekend festivals
● Lake View Market

TIPS

● Enjoy some winter fun
at Harbourfront's large
outdoor skating rink.
● Harbourfront Centre is
on the Waterfront Trail.

**This wonderful waterfront park can
occupy a whole day—biking, sailing,
canoeing, picnicking, shopping, watching
crafts-people at work—and even catching
a performance.**

Lakefront leisure Start at Queen's Quay
Terminal shopping mall (▷ 69), where specialty shops are housed in an attractive old
warehouse building. Several restaurants have
outside dining areas on the waterfront. Take the
lakeside walking trail to Bill Boyle Artport, stop-
ping at the Power Plant, a contemporary art
gallery, and The Harbourfront Centre behind it.
Outdoor areas for relaxation include Ontario
Square and Canada Square, both with mature
trees reflecting the natural landscape, and
Exhibition Common for outdoor exhibitions.

Clockwise from left: Queen's Quay Terminal interior and exterior; the lakefront and marina; Ontario Square; Bill Boyle Artport

At Bill Boyle Artport you'll find artisans at work and can purchase their glass, ceramics, jewelry, silk-screen designs, and metal sculptures in the adjacent store. York Quay's lakefront has a small pond, play area and the outdoor Concert Stage.

Rent a boat In good weather, Harbourfront is a great place to relax on the grass or people-watch from a waterfront café. Sail- and powerboats can be rented, or you can sign up for sailing lessons at Habourfront Centre Sailing and Powerboating (tel 416/203-3000).

Festivals and events Harbourfront holds more than 4,000 events, from the Milk International Children's Festival of the Arts to the International Festival of Authors in October, World Stage in April and the LunarFest in January.

THE BASICS

harbourfrontcentre.com

+ L9

✉ Harbourfront Centre, 235 Queens Quay West

☎ 416/973-4000

🕐 Bill Boyle Artport daily 10am–9pm. Power Plant Tue–Sun and holiday Mon 10–5, craft & design studio Tue–Sat 10–8, Sun 10–6 Queen's Quay Terminal daily 10am

🍽 Several

🚋 509 Harbourfront or 510 Spadina streetcar

♿ Very good

💲 Free

❓ Special events (ask at Bill Boyle Artport)

Toronto Islands

HIGHLIGHTS

● Centre Island
● Hanlan's Point
● View from Algonquin Island

TIPS

● If you're planning a picnic, don't bring alcohol—you need to order it in advance and pick it up from Centreville Catering (☎ 416/203-0405).
● Barbecue pits are available, but it's best to bring a portable charcoal barbecue in case they are all taken.

A mere 15-minute ferry ride takes you to this peaceful archipelago with meandering waterways, cycle paths and green lanes, which seems light years away from the bustling city you left behind.

A city retreat Originally a peninsula, inundated by the sea in a storm in 1858, the 14 Toronto Islands incorporate 243ha (600 acres) laced with waterways and inlets. People come to walk, cycle, play tennis, picnic, sit on the beach or go boating and stand-up paddleboarding.

The main areas These are Centre Island, Ward's Island and Hanlan's Point. The first is the busiest, with Centreville—an old-fashioned amusement park with an 1890s carousel, a flume ride and antique cars—and a small

working farm where children can pet the lambs and ride the ponies. From Centre Island a bridge crosses over the main watercourse (with boats for rent) to the arc of the former penin-sula, with Ward's Island to the east and Hanlan's Point to the west. Behind the shoreline, path-ways crisscross lawns dotted with trees, and there are barbecue pits, picnic tables and a playground. Other kids' attractions are the delightful Franklin Children's Garden and the William Meany Maze, where you can get lost among 1,200 shrubs. Ward's Island is the main residential spot, while the western area includes the Gibraltar Point Lighthouse, Artscape Gibraltar Point, with artists-in-residence and space for visiting artists, and—closest to the mainland—Billy Bishop Toronto airport. To explore, rent a bike or take the Island Tram Tour.

THE BASICS

➕ See map ▷ 94; Ferries M9

☎ Centreville 416/203-0405. Ferry 416/392-8193

🍴 Several options

🚋 509 Harbourfront or 510 Spadina (southbound) streetcars or Bay 6 bus to Ferry Docks

⛴ Approximately every 15 minutes in summer but less frequently in winter

♿ Few

💵 Ferry moderate

❓ Seasonal events

More to See

CORONATION PARK

toronto.ca/data/parks/prd/facilities/parks/index.html

Turn right at the end of Queen's Quay West to enjoy a wide expanse of parkland, with picnic areas, a bike trail, and softball pitches. A naval base occupies one corner, and the National and Alexandra Yacht Clubs have facilities on the shoreline. The World War II 50th Anniversary Memorial is accompanied by a group of commemorative tree plantings. At its western end, the park leads to the Toronto Inukshuk Park (formerly Battery Park), named for its Inukshuk monument in which large stones are piled into the shape of a man. This one stands 9m (30ft) high.

🞦 G9 ✉ 711 Lake Shore Boulevard 416/392-1111 🚋 509 Harbourfront, 511 Bathurst streetcars 🚈 Exhibition

EXHIBITION PLACE

explace.on.ca

Housing several exhibition and conference venues BMO Field (the 21,500-seat national soccer stadium), Ricoh Coliseum (home of the Toronto Marlies hockey team), Canada's Sport Hall of Fame and the Horse Palace riding academy, which also houses Toronto's police horses, there's plenty going, but the highlight is the annual Canadian National Exhibition (The Ex), from mid-August through early September. It includes exhibitors, attractions, midway rides, dog and horse shows, performances, an air show, shopping and food stands.

🞦 E8 ✉ Off Lake Shore Boulevard, Strachan Avenue and Dufferin Street 🕿 416/263-3000 or 3330 for Canadian National Exhibition 🚋 509 Harbourfront, 511 Bathurst streetcars 🚈 Exhibition

HTO PARK

toronto.ca/data/parks/prd/facilities/parks/index.html

This green space opened in 2007, with a name reflecting both the chemical composition of water (H_2O) and the city's familiar abbreviation (TO). Popular for its sandy

The Canadian National Exhibition

Queens Quay West

beach dotted with umbrellas, its imaginative landscaping adds interest as the sun casts its shadows, and artful lighting takes over the task after sunset.

➕ J9 ✉ Queen's Quay West near Rees Street 416/392-1111 🚋 509 Harbourfront, 510 Spadina streetcars

MARILYN BELL PARK

toronto.ca/data/parks/prd/facilities/parks/index.html

Out beyond Ontario Place and Exhibition Place, this park blends into the Lakeshore Boulevard Parklands, where locals walk their dogs or play tennis. Stroll on the lakefront boardwalk and ponder on the feat of the local girl after whom the park is named—at 16 years old, she was the first person to swim the 51km (32 miles) across Lake Ontario (in 1954, in a minute under 21 hours).

➕ B8 ✉ Lake Shore Boulevard West and British Columbia Road 416/392-1111 🚋 514 Dufferin Gate Loop streetcar 🚇 Exhibition

MARTIN GOODMAN TRAIL

waterfronttrail.org/Toronto

Toronto's lakeshore recreational trail is a 56km (nearly 35-mile) paved section of the Waterfront Trail, which stretches for 1,400km (870 miles) along Lake Ontario and beyond. Here, it runs through the city's resort area, linking the malls, entertainment venues, hotels, marina and green spaces. It's ideal for walking, cycling, in-line skating and skateboarding.

➕ C9 ✉ 416/392-1111 🚋 509 Harbourfront, 510 Spadina, 511 Bathurst streetcars

QUEENS QUAY WEST

Stretching from the bottom of Bay Street west to the foot of Bathurst, Queens Quay West has become a hotspot. In addition to giving access to attractions such as the Harbourfront Centre (▷ 64–65) and waterfront parks, it is lined by restaurants, hotels, and good specialty stores and malls.

➕ L9

REDPATH SUGAR MUSEUM

redpathsugars.com

If you have a half-hour or so to spare, this unusual little museum tells the story of the company that has refined and sold sugar and sugar products in Canada since 1853. It has displays about sugar cane, sugar beet, refining methods, the slave trade and social aspects of sugar.

➕ M8 ✉ 95 Queens Quay East ☎ 416/366-3561 🕐 Mon–Fri 10–12, 1–3.30 (call ahead) 🎫 Free 🚇 Union Station 🚌 6 ♿ Good

TORONTO MUSIC GARDEN

harbourfrontcentre.com/venues/torontomusicgarden

This 0.8ha (2-acre) park is a music garden in every sense, from its remarkable layout representing Bach's Suite No. 1 in G Major for Unaccompanied Cello—a visual collaboration between landscaper Julie Moir Messervy and cellist Yo-Yo Ma—to the free concerts staged here by the Harbourfront Centre in summer.

➕ H9 ✉ 479 Queens Quay West 416/392-1111 or 416/973-4000 🎫 Free 🚋 509 Harbourfront, 510 Spadina, 511 Bathurst streetcars

An Island Stroll

Take a ferry ride to discover an offshore haven, with parkland and beaches, bikes and boating, and spectacular views of the city.

DISTANCE: 2.5km (1.5 miles) **ALLOW:** 3 hours

START

TORONTO ISLANDS PIER
🚇 M9 🚌 Pier area

1 From the Jack Layton Ferry Terminal take the ferry to Centre Island (▷ 66). Cross the square to the island information booth in the far left corner then go left on the path that leads past Centreville to the bridge.

2 Cross the bridge and continue past the fountain, through the gardens to the beach and pier for a look southward over the lake.

3 Retrace your steps to the fountain, then turn right and follow the path to the boathouse. Loop around the back of the boathouse and continue to the pretty little church of St. Andrews by the Lake.

4 Continue on the same path, with occasional spectacular views across the water to the downtown sky-scrapers. Later pass the bridge (on your left) to Algonquin Island.

END

TORONTO ISLANDS PIER
🚇 M9 🚌 Pier area

8 As an alternative, from Ward's Island Beach you can turn right onto the boardwalk, which will take you back to the pier area.

7 From here you can take a ferry back to Centre Island and/or the mainland.

6 Turn left and then follow the path behind the beach, turning left at the end to loop around the residential area, then back along the northern shore to the Ward's Island Ferry Dock.

5 Walk past the Island Canoe Club building, then turn right to Ward's Island Beach.

Shopping

THE CENTRE SHOP

harbourfrontcentre.com

Within the Bill Boyle Artport, part of the Harbourfront Centre, this is a terrific crafts shop showcasing contemporary Canadian works. These include pieces made by the center's resident artists, who can often be seen at work in the studios here.

⊞ L9 ⊠ 235 Queens Quay West
☎ 416/973-4000 ⊕ Daily 11–6 🚇 Union
🚋 510 Spadina streetcar

KITCHEN TABLE

thekitchentable.ca

If you are looking for picnic supplies to take to the islands or one of the lakeshore parks, look no farther than this store with bakery and deli goods and fresh fruit. With five locations in downtown Toronto, supplies should be close at hand.

⊞ L8 ⊠ 10 Queens Quay West ☎ 416/778-4800 ⊕ Daily 6am–midnight 🚇 Union

LAKEVIEW MARKET

harbourfrontcentre.com

Stands selling crafts, jewelry, textiles and other goods from all over the world are set up on one of the quays at the Harbourfront Centre every summer weekend.

⊞ L9 ⊠ 235 Queens Quay West
☎ 416/973-4000 ⊕ Jul–early Sep, Sat–Sun from 8am 🚇 Union

LCBO

lcbo.com

The Liquor Control Board of Ontario store has a great selection of wines, including Canadian varieties, cool beers, spirits and the fixings for cocktails.

⊞ M8 ⊠ 2 Cooper Street, Queen's Quay
☎ 416/864-6863 ⊕ Mon–Sat 9am–10pm, Sun 12–6 🚇 Union

THE POWER PLANT

thepowerplant.org/Shop

If you enjoyed the exhibits in the art gallery, you'll enjoy the shop too. It has a range of artsy items, including artwork, books, posters, T-shirts and postcards.

⊞ L9 ⊠ 231 Queens Quay West
☎ 416/973-4949 ⊕ Tue–Sun and holiday Mon 10–5 (to 8 Thu) 🚇 Union 🚋 509 Harbourfront or 510 Spadina streetcars

QUEEN'S QUAY TERMINAL

brookfieldproperties.com

This upscale mall is a glittering space right on the lakeshore with an interesting selection of stores, including fashions, homewares, crafts, perfumes, toys and jewelry. Standouts include the Canadian Naturalist store, stocked full with quality Canadian-made clothing, crafts, and specialty foods, and the Museum of Inuit Art, with crafts for sale. There are several excellent restaurants with lakefront patios.

⊞ L9 ⊠ 207 Queens Quay West
☎ 416/203-0510 ⊕ Wed–Sat 10–9, Sun–Tue 10–6 (hours may change seasonally) 🚇 Union
🚋 510 Spadina streetcar

LAKESHORE MARKETS

The Lakeshore has a lively program of summer festivals and events, which often include shopping opportunities. The longest-running of these is the Waterfront Artisan Market, held every Saturday (11–8) from mid-May through early October at HTO Park, hosting more than 70 vendors. Many maintain social responsibility, from a commitment to sustainable and fair-trade materials to training and employing at-risk local youths to providing financial support to communities abroad. The Harbourfront Centre's cultural events include a Swedish Christmas Fair in late November.

Entertainment and Nightlife

BUDWEISER STAGE
livenation.com
A venue for rock, pop, jazz and other concerts, including some big-name acts, this Ontario Place arena has capacity for around 16,000, mostly open-air.
➕ D9 ✉ 909 Lake Shore Boulevard West ☎ 416/260-5600 🚇 Union 🚋 509 Harbourfront streetcar 🚃 Exhibition

CINESPHERE
The Ontario Place IMAX movie theater has the latest laser technology for the best sound and picture quality.
➕ D9 ✉ 955 Lake Shore Boulevard West ☎ 416/314-9900 🚇 Union 🚋 509 Harbourfront streetcar 🚃 Exhibition

FIRKIN ON HARBOUR
firkinpubs.com
With 20 draft beers on tap and a waterfall-facing patio courtyard, this British-style pub is perfect for a casual drink at the harborfront.
➕ M8 ✉ 10 Yonge Street ☎ 416/519-9949 🕐 Daily 11am–2am 🚇 Union

FLECK DANCE THEATRE
harbourfrontcentre.com
Contemporary and world dance performances regularly take place here in this modern theater.
➕ L9 ✉ 207 Queens Quay West ☎ 416/973-4000 box office, 416/973-4600 admin 🚇 Union 🚋 509 Harbourfront streetcar 🚃 Exhibition

HARBOURFRONT CENTRE THEATRE
harbourfrontcentre.com
A variety of concerts, world music and dance are staged at this fine theatre. Be sure to take a looks at *Waterglass*, a large-scale solar glass art exhibit by Canadian artist Sarah Hall.

➕ K9–L9 ✉ 235 Queens Quay West ☎ 416/973-4000 box office, 416/973-4600 admin 🚇 Union

MEDIEVAL TIMES DINNER & TOURNAMENT
medievaltimes.com
Jousting knights charge toward each other at high speed on Andalucian stallions while diners enjoy a multi-course feast preferred by costumed serfs. You'll need to book in advance.
➕ C8 ✉ Exhibition Place, 10 Dufferin Street ☎ 416/260-1234 or 1-866/935-6878 🚋 509 Harbourfront or 511 Bathurst streetcars 🚃 Exhibition

TORONTO MUSIC GARDEN
harbourfrontcentre.com
In this lovely garden, laid out on a musical theme, enjoy free summer concerts, from classical and world music to jazz and fiddle tunes.
➕ H/J9 ✉ 479 Queens Quay West ☎ 416/973-4000 box office, 416/973-4600 admin 🕐 Thu at 7, Sun at 4, late June–mid-Sep 🚇 Union 🚋 509 Harbourfront streetcar

---

STREET MUSIC

When the weather is suitable, there's nothing Canadians like more than to be outside, and that applies to many of their musicians, too. There are plenty of organized open-air concerts, with the Harbourfront Centre, Yonge-Dundas Square and the Distillery Historic District among popular venues, and you might even see a big-name local band playing on a makeshift stage on a city square (particularly if they have a cause to support). Equally appealing (usually) are the street musicians you come across unexpectedly—and you won't use the subway for long before you hear one of the 75 licenced acts scheduled to play down there.

Where to Eat

ALEXANDROS TAKE-OUT ($)

This hole-in-the-wall is handily located
by the waterfront of Westin Harbour
Castle is great value and serves a great
range of tasty Greek gyros, souvlakis
and crispy fries with feta cheese. Eat at
the nearby beach or on the little patio.

🔲 M8 ✉ 5 Queens Quay East ☎ 416/367-
0633 🕐 Daily 11 til late 🚃 509 Harbourfront
streetcar

AMSTERDAM BREWHOUSE ($$)

amsterdambeer.com/brewhouse

A lakefront location, lots of patio space,
beer brewed on the premises, and a
comprehensive menu makes this a
popular spot. Dishes range from house-
smoked meats and beer-battered fish to
Thai curries. Free brewery tours can also
be booked.

🔲 K9 ✉ 245 Queens Quay West
☎ 416/504-1020 🕐 Sun–Thu 11.30–11,
Fri–Sat 11.30am–2am 🚇 Union 🚃 509
Harbourfront streetcar

THE CAROUSEL CAFÉ ($)

On Centre Island, this lovely spot has
great views of the city and it's a good
place for a lazy, lingering lunch. There's
plenty of outdoor seating with umbrellas
for shade, and a tempting menu of well-
cooked dishes that will please the whole
family.

➕ Off map ✉ Centreville, Centre Island
☎ 416/203-0405 🕐 Varies seasonally; call for
details ⛴ Centre Island

HARBOUR SIXTY STEAKHOUSE ($$$$)

harbour60.com

Climb the stone steps to a gorgeous
baroque-inspired lobby to enjoy some
of the finest basic ingredients. Prime
beef, tuna, lobsters on ice, Atlantic
salmon and the best slow-roasted prime
rib beef in town. You can even hire an
opulent private dining room.

🔲 L8 ✉ 60 Harbour Street ☎ 416/777-
2111 🕐 Mon–Fri 11.30–5, Sat–Sun 5pm till
late 🚇 Union

PEARL HARBOURFRONT RESTAURANT ($$)

pearlharbourfront.ca

As the name suggests, this restaurant
offers a delightful lakefront dining experience, so reserve a window seat.
Authentic dishes include dim sum,
Peking duck, braised lobster, noodles,
and much more. There's another branch
in Bayview Shopping Centre.

🔲 L9 ✉ Queen's Quay Terminal, Main Level,
207 Queens Quay West ☎ 416/203-1233
🕐 Mon–Fri 11–3.30 and 5–10, Sat–Sun 10.30–
3.30 and 5–10 🚇 Union

PICNIC PLACES

With all the fantastic parks lining the lakeshore, there's no shortage of perfect places
to spread a blanket and lay out your feast.
Many of the parks have picnic tables, too.
Take the ferry over to the Toronto Islands
and you will find not only tables, but also
barbecue pits, though they get taken very
quickly. If you take your own barbecue,
only small, charcoal burning types are
allowed on the ferry (they won't carry
alcohol either). You can get supplies at the
excellent Kitchen Table (▷ 71) or from
the big Loblaws supermarket on Queens
Quay East.

Queen's Park and Midtown

Powerhouses of government and learning are concentrated around Queen's Park, between the busy thoroughfares of College and Bloor streets. Farther north, streets of heritage homes fill the Annex, leading to a remarkable piece of architecture.

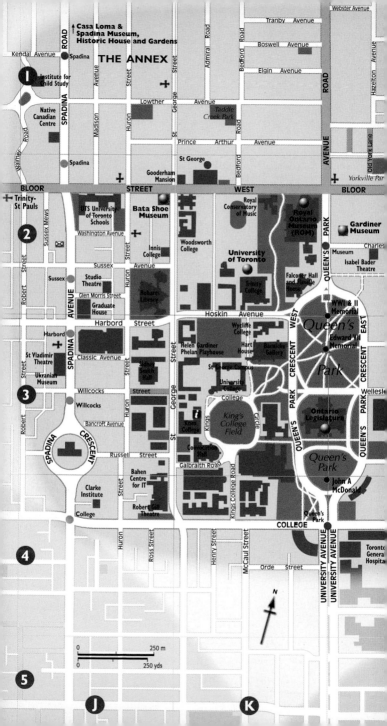

Bata Shoe Museum

HIGHLIGHTS

● Mold of Homo sapiens footprint made 3.7 million years ago
● 4,500-year-old wooden sandals
● 2,000-year-old espadrilles
● 500-year-old footwear of a Mayan boy sacrifice
● 7.5cm (3in) "gin lien" for bound feet

TIP

● Allow more time than you think you are going to need and bring the children—there's lots of fun to be had here.

Housed in a structure resembling a shoe box, there are more than 13,000 items in the displays of footwear past and present.

More than just shoes The main exhibit traces the history of shoes from a footprint made 3.7 million years ago in Tanzania to the extraordinary shoes of today. Three other galleries have changing exhibitions on various themes. The sheer variety of beautiful and truly striking footwear is amazing. Each display is set against cutouts reflecting the particular period or geographic location. There are all kinds of ceremonial shoes: leather sandals with gilded images worn by the King of Kumasi in Ghana for state occasions; wedding shoes from various cultures; and lacquered and painted shoes worn to Shinto shrines in Japan. The museum

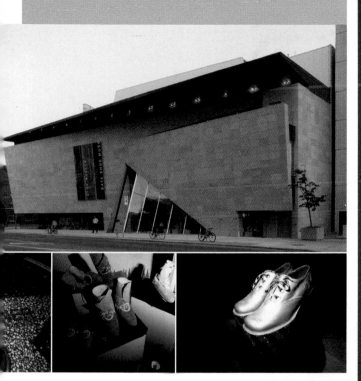

Clockwise from left: The hard-to-miss Bata Shoe Museum; interior staircase; exterior view; a pair of Elton John's shoes; sheepskin boots and moccasins; one of actress Lana Turner's sandals

is a gold mine of little-known facts; for instance, that Elizabeth I was in part responsible for the foot problems caused by high heels because she popularized them in an attempt to appear taller. The style was limited to the elite, hence the term "well-heeled." Toe length also indicated social status; in England, in the mid-14th century, anyone earning less than 40 livres was not allowed to wear pointed toes, a nobleman could wear shoes with toes 61cm (24in) long, and a prince could wear toes of any length.

Celebrity footwear The collection includes shoes worn by famous people, including Picasso's mock-zebra lace-ups, Elton John's 30cm (12in) high platform shoes, one of John Lennon's "Beatle Boots" from the early 1960s and Marilyn Monroe's red leather pumps.

THE BASICS

batashoemuseum.ca

✠ J2

✉ 327 Bloor Street West

☎ 416/979-7799

🕓 Mon–Wed, Fri–Sat 10–5, Thu 10–8, Sun 12–5

🚇 St. George

♿ Excellent

💵 Moderate; by donation Thu 5–8

❓ Lectures, guided tours, family events, folkloric events

Casa Loma

Interior views (left); looking toward Casa Loma (right)

A magnificent and whimsical place with its Elizabethan chimneys, Rhenish turrets and secret passageways, Casa Loma is Sir Henry Pellatt's idea of what constituted European aristocratic splendor.

Canadian-style splendor A striking mix of 18th-century Scottish baronial and 20th-century Fox, Casa Loma is a rich man's folly. It cost $3.5 million to build, yet after real estate changes was valued at $27,305 only 10 years later. Between 1911 and 1914 Pellatt created this fantasy home, importing Scottish stonemasons and Italian woodcarvers, then spending an additional $1.5 million furnishing the 98 rooms. A hammerbeam ceiling covers the 20m (66ft) high Great Hall; three artisans took three years to carve the paneling in the Oak Room; splendid bronze doors lead to a marble conservatory crowned with a stained-glass dome. Modern luxuries included an elevator, a private telephone system, marble swimming pool, 15 baths and 5,000 electric lights. A tunnel runs out to the stables, where, amid Spanish tile and mahogany, horses' names were displayed in 18-carat gold letters above each stall.

The bubble bursts The son of a stockbroker, Pellatt went into the brokerage business after college, and amassed $17 million. Still in his twenties, he founded Toronto's first hydroelectric power company, but his wealth evaporated in 1920 when electric power was ruled a public utility. Pellatt died penniless in 1939.

The centilevered exterior (left); a ceramic sculpture on display (right)

Gardiner Museum

This outstanding museum is the only one in Canada dedicated to ceramic art. Its collections comprise more than 3,000 pieces, and include Ancient American, Chinese, English, Italian, other European, Japanese and contemporary works.

Colorful earthenware The marvelous collection of pre-Columbian pottery includes figures and vessels dating from 3000BC to the 16th century AD, ranging from Mexico to Peru. Among them are some remarkable pieces by the Olmecs, red clay Nayarit figures, Zacatecan-style male statuettes with horns, smiling figures from Nopiloa, Los Cerros, or Isla de Sacrificios, fine orange and plumbate ware of the Mayans, and Aztec objects. The next great period of ceramic art is represented by colorful Italian majolica from the 15th and 16th centuries, and there is a selection of English tin-glazed earthenware, including blue-and-white Delftware.

Delicate porcelain The porcelain collection is extraordinary. It includes figures by Meissen's sculptor-potter Joachim Kändler and some prime examples of Sèvres. English porcelain is well represented, from the early softpaste pieces manufactured at Chelsea and Bow to the later bone china that was invented by Josiah Spode. The collection also features 120 figures from the *commedia dell'arte* and 100 mid-18th-century scent bottles, ranging from early Meissen to highly decorated rococo versions from various sources.

THE BASICS

gardinermuseum.com

🏠 L2

🖂 111 Queen's Park

☎ 416/586-8080

🕐 Mon–Thu 10–6, Fri 10–9, Sat–Sun 10–5

🍴 Museum

♿ Very good

🎟 Moderate; half-price Fri 4–9

❓ Tours, lectures

HIGHLIGHTS

● Olmec figures
● Smiling figures
● Majolica
● *Commedia dell'arte* figures
● Scent bottles

Royal Ontario Museum

HIGHLIGHTS

● Dinosaurs
● Stair of Wonders
● Spirit House
● China Galleries
● Middle East and South Asia
● The Americas Gallery

TIPS

● Friday Night Live events (seasonal) have live music, food and fun activities.
● School groups tend to visit in the morning.

As one of North America's great museums and Canada's largest, the Royal Ontario Museum (ROM) opened in 1914 and continues to be one of the biggest draws in the city today.

Michael Lee-Chin Crystal This startling work of modern architecture literally bursts out of the century-old walls of the original museum in great prisms that tower over Bloor Street, enabling passersby to look up and see exhibits in the halls above. Inside, its seven galleries have crazy angles and sweeping curves and are bathed in natural light. A fine-dining restaurant has incredible views. Threading up through the building is the Stair of Wonders, highlighting more than 1,000 unusual exhibits, including natural history items and applied arts.

Clockwise from left: Entrance to the museum; a highly decorated ceiling; dinosaur skeletons; interactive exhibits

The collections The ROM boasts around 6 million objects in its varied collections, which incorporate world cultures and natural history. The Chinese collections are particularly oustanding, and include galleries devoted to temple art, sculpture, decorative arts and other historic objects. Canada is represented in the excellent Sigmund Samuel and Daphne Cockwell galleries, the latter focusing on First Peoples' culture and art. Other exhibitions range from ancient European civilizations to delicate Japanese ceramics.

Other exhibits There's a world-class collection of dinosaur skeletons and fossils, and the bat exhibit, which includes a walk-through bat cave diorama. Young visitors will love the three hands-on galleries, including a digital suite.

THE BASICS

rom.on.ca

✚ K2

✉ 100 Queen's Park

☎ 416/586-8000

🕐 Daily 10–5.30, also Fri from 7pm late Sep–late Nov

🍴 Food Café

Ⓢ St. George, Museum

♿ Excellent

✋ Moderate

More to See

BLOOR-YORKVILLE

Populated in the 1960s by budding icons of the pop music and literary worlds, this neighborhood has gentrified beyond recognition into a glitzy shopping destination. Exclusive fashion stores include Burberry, Tiffany & Co, Prada, Louis Vuitton and many more world-famous designer names. Flagship stores for upscale department stores, such as Holt Renfrew and Harry Rosen, are also here, along with some mid-range stores.

➕ L1 ✉ Bloor Street West, Davenport Road and Yonge Street 🚇 Bloor-Yonge

ONTARIO LEGISLATURE

ontla.on.ca

For anyone fascinated by government, time spent in the public gallery when parliament is in session might be rewarded with some lively exchanges or at least an insight into how laws affecting 14 million Ontarians are passed. The 1893 building is a massive Romanesque Revival structure of reddish-brown sandstone, finely decorated inside. If the house is not sitting, take a guided tour of the opulent building or Queen's Park, if they're on offer. Expect a security check, including showing a piece of government-issued ID for visitors over 16 years.

➕ K3 ✉ Queen's Park ☎ 416/325-7500, 416/325-0061 for tour information 🕐 Victoria Day weekend–Labour Day daily 8–4, rest of year Mon–Fri 8.30–6 🍴 Cafeteria, dining room 🚇 Queen's Park, Museum ♿ Good 💷 Free ❓ Public gallery viewing when parliament is in session

ROSEDALE

If you truly want to escape the city then visit Rosedale, Toronto's most affluent and elegant neighborhood, with large, beautiful homes owned by the city's movers and shakers. Many of the buildings, which mostly date from the mid-19th century to the 1920s, are listed Heritage Properties on large, landscaped lots around pleasant leafy streets.

➕ M1 🚇 Rosedale

Yorkville

Spadina House

SPADINA MUSEUM: HISTORIC HOUSE AND GARDENS

toronto.ca

This fine mansion, with its original furnishings and gas lights, was once at the heart of an estate with its own golf course. After an entertaining introductory film, there's an excellent guided tour that really brings the Austin family to life, with anecdotes and showing personal possessions of the family. Afterward, you can take a stroll in the lovely gardens.

➕ Off map at J1 ✉ 285 Spadina Road ☎ 416/392-6910 🕐 Apr–Labour Day Tue–Sun and holiday Mon 12–5; Sep–Jan Tue–Fri 12–4, Sat–Sun and Thanksgiving Mon 12–5; Jan–Mar Sat–Sun 12–5 🚇 Dupont 🚹 Good 💵 Inexpensive

UNIVERSITY OF TORONTO

utoronto.ca

Wandering around the campus, with its stately buildings and pleasant gardens, you'll be following the footsteps of the team of scientists who discovered insulin, a couple of prime ministers, and other famous alumni including Margaret Atwood, Farley Mowat, Atom Egoyan and Donald Sutherland. The architecture is an intriguing mix of Gothic, Romanesque Revival and modern. Don't miss the Canadian art collection in the Justina M. Barnicke Gallery in Hart House.

➕ K2 ✉ West of Queen's Park ☎ 416/978-2011 🍴 Gallery Grill in Hart House and cafeterias in campus buildings 🚇 Museum 🚃 Queen's Park streetcar; 506 Carlton streetcar 🚹 Good 💵 Free ❓ Tours year round

YORKVILLE BRANCH LIBRARY

torontopubliclibrary.ca

Built in 1907 as the first of four libraries for the Toronto Public Library system, the Yorkville Branch is in classical Beaux Arts style and is now the system's oldest library. It's home to a local history and theater collection, and an Art Exhibit Space.

➕ M1 ✉ 22 Yorkville Avenue ☎ 416/393-7660 🕐 Mon–Thu 9–8.30, Fri–Sat 9–5 🚇 Bloor-Yonge

University of Toronto

Midtown Hits

Yet another facet of Toronto: the stately buildings of parliament and academia, the ROM, and upscale shopping in Yorkville.

DISTANCE: 3km (1.8 miles) **ALLOW:** 2 hours

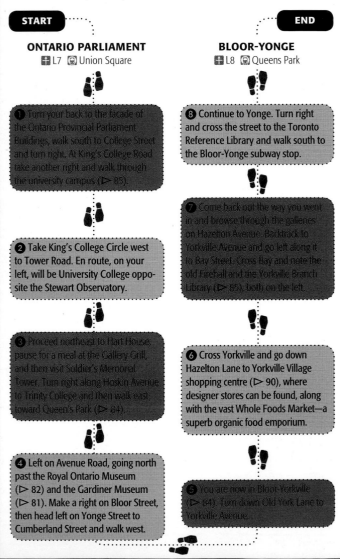

START

ONTARIO PARLIAMENT
🚇 L7 ⬛ Union Square

❶ Turn your back to the facade of the Ontario Provincial Parliament Buildings, walk south to College Street and turn right. At King's College Road take another right and walk through the university campus (▷ 85).

❷ Take King's College Circle west to Tower Road. En route, on your left, will be University College opposite the Stewart Observatory.

❸ Proceed northeast to Hart House, pause for a meal at the Gallery Grill, and then visit Soldier's Memorial Tower. Turn right along Hoskin Avenue to Trinity College and then walk east toward Queen's Park (▷ 84).

❹ Left on Avenue Road, going north past the Royal Ontario Museum (▷ 82) and the Gardiner Museum (▷ 81). Make a right on Bloor Street, then head left on Yonge Street to Cumberland Street and walk west.

END

BLOOR-YONGE
🚇 L8 ⬛ Queens Park

❽ Continue to Yonge. Turn right and cross the street to the Toronto Reference Library and walk south to the Bloor-Yonge subway stop.

❼ Come back out the way you went in and browse through the galleries on Hazelton Avenue. Backtrack to Yorkville Avenue and go left along it to Bay Street. Cross Bay and note the old Firehall and the Yorkville Branch Library (▷ 85), both on the left.

❻ Cross Yorkville and go down Hazelton Lane to Yorkville Village shopping centre (▷ 90), where designer stores can be found, along with the vast Whole Foods Market—a superb organic food emporium.

❺ You are now in Bloor-Yorkville (▷ 84). Turn down Old York Lane to Yorkville Avenue.

Shopping

GRIGORIAN

grigorian.com

This is a store for the devoted music lover. It contains a stunning collection of classical music and jazz CDs.

➕ J6 ✉ 70 Yorkville Avenue ☎ 416/922-6477 🕐 Mon–Thu and Sat 10–6, Fri 10–7, Sun 12–5 🚇 Bloor-Yonge

HARRY ROSEN

harryrosen.com

Four floors of fashions for men, including all the top men's designers—Armani, Samuelsohn, Canali and Hugo Boss.

➕ J6 ✉ 82 Bloor Street West ☎ 416/972-0556 🕐 Mon–Wed and Sat 10–7, Thu–Fri 10–9, Sun 12–7 🚇 Bloor-Yonge or Bay

HOLT RENFREW CENTRE

holtrenfrew.com

As well as the Holt Renfrew store, with designer fashion, salon, spa, perfumes, and café, retailers include Femme de Carriere, Aritzia and Ginkgo Health Shop.

➕ J6 ✉ 50 Bloor Street West ☎ 416/922-2333 🕐 Mon–Wed and Sat 10–8, Thu–Fri 10–9, Sun 11–7 🚇 St. George

KUMARI'S

kumaris.ca

For women's clothes that will turn heads, check out the richly colored cashmere and silk creations here. It's cheerful, but not cheap.

➕ L2 ✉ 25 Bellair Street ☎ 416/324-9830 Mon–Sat 11–6, Sun 12–5 🚇 Bay

M0851

m0851.com

Minimalist, high-quality leather bags, accessories, coats and outerwear, designed and manufactured in Montréal.

➕ K1 ✉ 38 Avenue Road ☎ 416/920-4001 🕐 Mon–Wed and Sat 10–6, Thu–Fri 10–7, Sun 12–6 🚇 St. George

PUSATERI'S FINE FOODS

pusateris.com

A mouth-watering array of global gourmet treats, including chef-prepared picnic foods, luxury confectionary and quality meat from the in-store butcher.

➕ L1 ✉ 57 Yorkville Avenue ☎ 416/925-0583 🕐 Mon–Wed, Sat 7.30am–8pm, Thu–Fri 7.30am–9pm; Sun 7.30am–7pm 🚇 Bay

ROLO

rolostore.com

If it's unique gadgets and gifts you are looking for, head to tiny, friendly Rolo for a wide assortment of novelty items.

➕ L1 ✉ 24 Bellair Street ☎ 416/920-0100 🕐 Mon 10.30–6, Tue–Fri 10.30–7, Sat 10.30–6, Sun 12–5 🚇 Bay

SILVERBRIDGE

silverbridge.com

Marvelously sculptured pieces of sterling silver: necklaces, bracelets, rings and earrings, cuff links and key holders.

➕ J6 ✉ 162 Cumberland Street ☎ 416/923-2591 🚇 Bay

WILLIAM ASHLEY

williamashley.com

All the great names in china and glass plus home decor and kitchenware.

➕ J6 ✉ 131 Bloor Street West ☎ 416/964-2900 🕐 Mon–Wed, Sat 10–6, Thu–Fri 10–8, Sun 12–5 🚇 Bloor-Yonge

YORKVILLE VILLAGE SHOPPING CENTRE

yorkvillevillage.com

The former Hazelton Lanes has a classy roster of retailers and a summer artisan market. The modern art gallery, Galerie de Bellefeuille, is a highlight.

➕ L1 ✉ 55 Avenue Road ☎ 416/968-8600 🕐 Mon–Sat 10–6 (to 7 Thu), Sun 12–5 (individual store hours may vary) 🚇 Bay

Entertainment and Nightlife

BUDDIES IN BAD TIMES THEATRE

buddiesinbadtimes.com

Renowned for staging first-rate new plays on LGBTQ themes and for its friendly, inclusive atmosphere, Buddies also has late-night dancing (for ages 19+ with photo ID) on Saturday nights.

🚇 M3 ✉ 12 Alexander Street ☎ 416/975-8555 🚊 College, Wellesley

DBAR

dbartoronto.com

In this elegant cocktail lounge with a tempting appetizer menu, you can expect celebrity spotting and excellent service. Check out the terrace.

🚇 L1 ✉ Four Seasons Hotel, 60 Yorkville Avenue ☎ 416/964-0411 🚊 Bay

FREE TIMES CAFÉ

freetimescafe.com

Go to hear the folk acoustic entertainment. Monday is open house, so bring your instrument and sign up at 7pm.

🚇 H4 ✉ 320 College Street between Major and Roberts ☎ 416/967-1078 🚌 507 Carlton, College streetcars

HART HOUSE THEATRE

harthouse.ca

The performing arts venue of the University of Toronto showcases Canada's talent.

🚇 K3 ✉ 7 Hart House Circle, University of Toronto ☎ 416/978-8849 🚊 Queen's Park, Museum

LEE'S PALACE

leespalace.com

You'll hear the latest in rock music here, including up-and-coming British bands. It's also home to local alternative bands and has a dance bar with a DJ.

🚇 H2 ✉ 529 Bloor Street West ☎ 416/532-1598 🚊 Bathurst

PEGASUS BAR

pegasusonchurch.com

This lively place in Toronto's gay village is for everyone, with music and dancing that's less frantic than in the nearby clubs. You can also play pool and darts, or just enjoy a drink.

🚇 M3 ✉ 489B Church Street ☎ 416/927-8832 🚊 Wellesley

PHOENIX CONCERT THEATRE

A full roster of live bands and a good sound system to draw crowds. It's mostly standing only, but some seats are available.

🚇 N3 ✉ 410 Sherbourne Street ☎ 416/323-1251 🚊 Wellesley or College

TRANZAC

tranzac.org

The Toronto Australia New Zealand Club is a nonprofit venue promoting music, theater and the arts. There's something on most evenings, including folk, jazz and indie, often with no cover charge.

🚇 H2 ✉ 292 Brunswick Avenue ☎ 416/923-8137 🚊 Spadina

LGBTQ

To get a fix on the scene, pick up *Xtra!* or go to **Glad Day Bookshop** (🚇 K6 ✉ 598a Yonge Street ☎ 416/961-4161, gladdaybookshop.com), which also hosts events. Also check dailyxtra.com and seetorontonow.com/toronto-diversity. The area around the Church Street and Wellesley Street intersection is known as the Church & Wellesley Gay Village, with lots of clubs and bars, including **Woody's** (🚇 K7 ✉ 467 Church Street ☎ 416/972-0887); **Statlers** (🚇 M3 ✉ 487 Church Street ☎ 416/922-0487) and **Crews & Tangos** (🚇 M3 ✉ 508 Church Street ☎ 647/349-7469).

Where to Eat

PRICES

Prices are approximate, based on a 3-course meal for one person.

$$$$	over $80
$$$	$60–$80
$$	$35–$60
$	under $35

COMO EN CASA ($)

comoencasa.ca

Welcoming and easy-going, this authentic Mexican restaurant serves generous portions at reasonable prices.

🔳 M3 ✉ 565 Yonge Street ☎ 647/748-6666 🕐 Mon–Fri 11–9, Sat noon–9 🚇 Wellesley

FIERAMOSCA ($$)

fieramoscatoronto.com

This trattoria delivers good Southern Italian dishes. The leafy patio is perfect for sunnier days, and there's also a private dining room with a terrace upstairs.

🔳 K1 ✉ 36A Prince Arthur Avenue ☎ 416/323-0636 🕐 Mon–Fri 11–3, Sat–Sun 5–11 🚇 St. George

FUTURE BISTRO ($)

futurebistro.ca

A European-style cafeteria, this eatery is beloved for its large portions of goulash and schnitzel sandwiches.

🔳 H3 ✉ 483 Bloor Street West ☎ 416/922-5875 🕐 Sun–Thu 8am–1am, Fri–Sat 8am–2am 🚇 Spadina or Bathurst

JOSO'S ($$$)

josos.com

This is the best place for fresh fish in Toronto. Select your own fish from the tray and it will be grilled, steamed, poached or cooked to order. The calamari are legendary.

🔳 Off map at L1 ✉ 202 Davenport Road (just east of Avenue Road) ☎ 416/925-1903

🕐 Mon–Fri 11.30–2.30 and from 5.30 Sat 🚇 Bay 🚌 Bus 6

MORTON'S ($$$$)

mortons.com

In an upscale environment that you might be sharing with a celebrity or two, this steakhouse serves top-quality prime beef. There's lots of seafood on the menu too, and sides that could create a satisfying vegetarian meal.

🔳 K1 ✉ Park Hyatt Hotel, 4 Avenue Road ☎ 416/925-0648 🕐 Mon–Fri 5.30–11, Sat 5–11, Sun 5–10 🚇 Bay or Museum

MUSEUM TAVERN ($$)

museumtavern.ca

American pub food that comes with a welcome twist: elk sliders, duck buns, beef short-rib poutine, truffled perogies. There are some classic menu items too, and a good view of the Royal Ontario Museum from the patio.

🔳 K2 ✉ 208 Bloor Street West ☎ 416/920-0110 🕐 Daily 11.30–late 🚇 St. George

WOW SUSHI ($)

wowsushitoronto.com

It may be tiny, but this sushi restaurant, owned by two brothers, has skilled chefs behind the counter. Try the Rainbow roll or the Japango roll.

🔳 M2 ✉ 11 Charles Street West ☎ 416/923-1888 🕐 Daily 11–10 🚇 Yonge

AGE LIMITS

The legal drinking age in Ontario is 19, and young people should be prepared to show government-issued photo ID because entry and/or alcohol service can be refused. Restrictions also apply within LCBO (Liquor Control Board of Ontario) stores—no-one under 19 may handle alcoholic products, even to help carry items to the cashier.

In the Greater Toronto area and beyond, you will find first-class culture, delightful and lively heritage towns and one of the greatest wonders of the natural world.

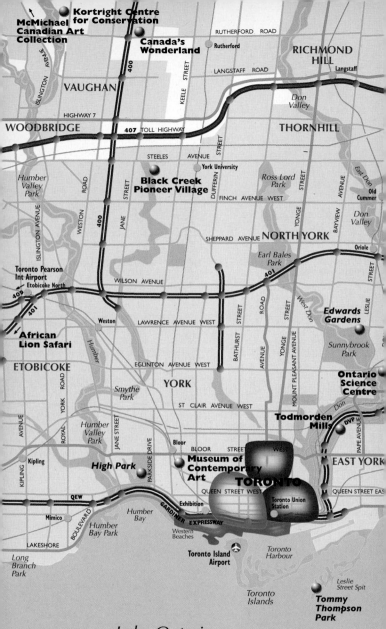

Kortright Centre for Conservation

McMichael Canadian Art Collection

Canada's Wonderland

RUTHERFORD ROAD

Rutherford

RICHMOND HILL

Langstaff

LANGSTAFF ROAD

VAUGHAN

Don Valley

HIGHWAY 7

WOODBRIDGE

407 TOLL HIGHWAY

THORNHILL

STEELES AVENUE

York University

Black Creek Pioneer Village

Ross Lord Park

Humber Valley Park

FINCH AVENUE WEST

Old Cummer

SHEPPARD AVENUE **NORTH YORK**

Don Valley

Earl Bales Park

Oriole

Toronto Pearson Int Airport

Etobicoke North

WILSON AVENUE

401

Edwards Gardens

Weston

LAWRENCE AVENUE WEST

Sunnybrook Park

African Lion Safari

ETOBICOKE

EGLINTON AVENUE WEST

Smythe Park

YORK

Ontario Science Centre

ST CLAIR AVENUE WEST

Humber Valley Park

Kipling

High Park

Bloor

BLOOR STREET WEST

Museum of Contemporary Art

TORONTO

Todmorden Mills

Don

DVP

EAST YORK

QUEEN STREET WEST

QUEEN STREET EAST

QEW

Exhibition

Toronto Union Station

Mimico

GARDINER EXPRESSWAY

Humber Bay

Western Beaches

Toronto Island Airport

Toronto Harbour

LAKESHORE

Humber Bay Park

Long Branch Park

Toronto Islands

Leslie Street Spit

Tommy Thompson Park

Lake Ontario

0   5 km

0   3 mile

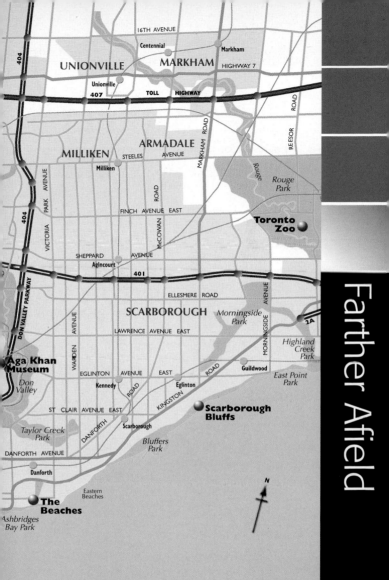

16TH AVENUE

Centennial

MARKHAM

Markham

HIGHWAY 7

UNIONVILLE

Unionville

404

407 TOLL HIGHWAY

RESOR ROAD

ARMADALE

MARKHAM ROAD

MILLIKEN

STEELES AVENUE

Milliken

Rouge Park

PARK AVENUE

VICTORIA AVENUE

404

McCOWAN ROAD

FINCH AVENUE EAST

Toronto Zoo

SHEPPARD AVENUE

Agincourt

401

DON VALLEY PARKWAY

ELLESMERE ROAD

MORNINGSIDE AVENUE

2A

SCARBOROUGH

Morningside Park

AVENUE

LAWRENCE AVENUE EAST

Highland Creek Park

WARDEN AVENUE

MORNINGSIDE

Aga Khan Museum

EGLINTON AVENUE EAST

Guildwood

East Point Park

Don Valley

Kennedy

KINGSTON ROAD

ROAD

Eglinton

Scarborough Bluffs

ST CLAIR AVENUE EAST

DANFORTH

Scarborough

Taylor Creek Park

Bluffers Park

DANFORTH AVENUE

Danforth

Eastern Beaches

N

The Beaches

Ashbridges Bay Park

Lake Ontario

Black Creek Pioneer Village

TOP 25

Inside the weaver's shop (left); traditional general store (right)

THE BASICS

blackcreek.ca
⊞ See map ▷ 92
✉ 1000 Murray Ross Parkway, North York
☎ 416/736-1733
🕓 Apr–Jun Mon–Fri 10–4, Sat–Sun 11–5; Jul–early Sep Mon–Fri 10–5, Sat–Sun 11–5; early Sep–Dec Mon–Fri 10–4, Sat–Sun 11–4.30. Closed Jan–Mar
🍴 Restaurant and snack bar
🚇 Pioneer Village
♿ Good
💰 Moderate

HIGHLIGHTS

● Coopering
● Tinsmithing
● Flour milling
● Heritage gardens
● Laskay Emporium and Post Office
● Half Way House

This living-history park re-creates life in a 19th-century Ontario village. Leave behind the stresses of modern times and step back into the past.

Family farm Black Creek is built around the Stong family farm—their first log house (1816), smokehouse and barn (1825), and a second clapboard home that they built in 1832. Even the sheep and hogs are imported English breeds that would have been familiar to the 19th-century pioneers.

Village life The village consists of 40 mid-19th-century buildings. Seeds are sold at the Laskay Emporium store, along with old-fashioned candy and brooms made in the village. Half Way House Inn and Restaurant (it stood halfway between York and Scarborough) is a stagecoach tavern. Loaves are baked here daily in the old hearth oven. A working brewery uses traditional methods and offers tastings. It's all brought to life by the artisans, who take delight in passing on their skills and knowledge. The cooper hunches over the barrel stove compressing staves to make barrels and pails held together without a single nail. Others demonstrate tinsmithing, weaving, cabinetmaking, blacksmithing, clockmaking and printing. Dickson's Hill School is a one-room schoolhouse that has separate entrances for boys and girls. The gardens include a herb garden with 42 types of herb, the weaver's shop's colorful dye garden and a medicinal garden.

Thrills for all ages at Canada's Wonderland

Canada's Wonderland

Rollercoaster addicts will revel in Canada's Wonderland because it contains no less than 16 coasters. The park has more than 65 rides and 200 attractions—adding new thrillers every year to keep the locals coming back.

Gut-wrenchers The latest ride is Lumberjack, two gigantic axe-shaped pendulums swinging up to 22m (72ft) high. The Leviathon reaches speeds of 148kmh (92 mph) and includes an 80-degree-angle drop from its summit of 93m (306ft), while Shockwave spins and loops riders through 360 degrees. The daredevil Drop Tower takes riders 70m (230ft) up into the air and then drops them in a 96kph (60mph) free fall. The Xtreme Skyflyer, lifting riders 45m (150ft), delivers all the thrills of skydiving and hang-gliding. Other favorites include the inverted looping jet coaster, Flight Deck, and the Backlot Stunt Coaster.

Water plus Perfect for a hot day, Splash Works is the 16ha (40-acre) water park, with an extra-large wave pool generating white caps, 18 water slides, including the Muskoka Plunge, an 18-meter (60-foot) set of four superfast slides with S-bends and 306-degree loops. There's also a fun aquatic jungle gym that's suitable for younger or more timid children. Other gentler rides include an antique carousel, while younger children will have fun in Kidzville and Planet Snoopy. The park has live shows, special events, and fireworks in the summer.

THE BASICS

canadaswonderland.com

⊞ See map ▷ 92

⊠ 9580 Jane Street Vaughan. Take Hwy 400 to Rutherford Road

☎ 905/832-8131

⏲ Early May–early Oct daily. Hours vary throughout the season

🍴 Many outlets

🚇 Yorkdale or York Mills then the Wonderland Express GO bus

🚌 165A

♿ Few

💵 Expensive (One Price Passport)

HIGHLIGHTS

● Leviathon
● Splash Works
● White Water Canyon
● Backlot Stunt Coaster
● Halloween events

TIPS

● Buying tickets online is cheaper; the two-day pass is a good value, and late-afternoon admission is almost half price.
● You can't picnic inside the park, but there's an area outside the front gate.

High Park

Grenadier Pond (left); Sakura cherry trees in full bloom (right)

THE BASICS

➕ See map ▷ 92
✉ 1873 Bloor Street West
☎ 416/392-6916 for Colborne Lodge, 416/721-2012 for trackless train, 416/392-7807 for swimming pool
🕐 Park always accessible; Colborne Lodge mid-Jan–Feb and Apr Fri–Sun 12–4, Mar Thu–Sun 12–4 (Mar break daily 12.30–4), May–Aug Tue–Sun 12–5, Sep Sat–Sun 12–5, Oct–Dec Tue–Sun 12–4
🍴 Grenadier Café
Ⓖ High Park
🚋 506 Carlton or 508 Lakeshore streetcars
♿ Good
💵 Free; Colborne Lodge inexpensive; trackless train inexpensive

HIGHLIGHTS

● Cherry Blossom Festival
● Hillside Gardens
● Colborne Lodge

TIP

● If you are planning a picnic, note that barbecues are not allowed in the park.

Toronto is a city with many parks but this is the largest and one of the loveliest, a haven of natural landscapes where you can imagine yourself in the countryside. The picnic areas, playground, zoo and sports amenities make for a full day out.

An urban haven Covering more than 160ha (nearly 400 acres), the park offers lots of breathing space. Its rich ecology includes a rare section of Black Oak Savannah, all that's left of the sand prairie systems that once dominated the southern Ontario landscape.

Activities for all There's plenty to do and see, from tennis, swimming and guided nature walks to the Shakespeare in High Park and other performances at the amphitheater. For children, the Jamie Bell Adventure Park, by the duck pond, is enthralling, with its fairy-tale wooden turrets, slides and rope swings, and there's also a small free zoo, with cattle, llamas, bison, and deer. To explore the easy way, trackless trains circulate (weather permitting), letting passengers off at various points, including at the glorious Hillside Gardens and Grenadier Pond.

Colborne Lodge At the southern end of the park, this was the home of the Howard family, who founded the park. It is now preserved as a museum, with its original furnishings, and guided tours are offered. Special events include an Easter egg hunt, a harvest festival and Christmas tours.

The cafeteria (left); inside the building housing the collection (right)

McMichael Canadian Art Collection

Tom Thomson and the artists known as the Group of Seven took their easels north and painted what they saw, revealing the northern wilderness to the rest of the world. Their revolutionary works are displayed in a woodland setting.

Artist by artist The permanent collection chronicles the development of the Group of Seven, Canada's most influential landscape school, formed in the 1920s, and their contemporaries, Tom Thomson, David Milne, and Emily Carr. The works of each of the group's artists are hung together to show how each evolved. All the favorites are here: the brilliantly colored canvases of Lake Superior by Alexander Young Jackson; Algonquin Park as seen by Tom Thomson; the rural villages depicted by Alfred Joseph Casson; the Killarney Provincial Park rendered by Franklin Carmichael; the starkly beautiful icebergs captured by Lawren Harris; portraits of British Columbia by Frederick Horsman Varley; and the portrayal of northwestern forests and First Nations villages by Emily Carr. One series of paintings portrays the Seven working outdoors. The most appealing depicts Franklin Carmichael sketching at Grace Lake.

First Nations and Inuit art Paintings, drawings, prints and sculptures by contemporary First Nations and Inuit artists—Norval Morrisseau, Daphne Odjig, Alex Janvier, Bill Reid—are displayed in changing shows drawn from the gallery's permanent collection.

THE BASICS

mcmichael.com

➕ See map ▷ 92

✉ 10365 Islington Avenue, Kleinburg

☎ 905/893-1121 or 1-888/213-1121

🕐 Daily 10–5 May–Oct, Tue–Sun 10–4 Nov–Apr

🍴 Cafeteria

🚇 Yonge–University–Spadina to bus 60, then bus 13

♿ Good

💲 Moderate

❓ Daily tours at 12.30pm and 2pm

HIGHLIGHTS

● Emily Carr's *Corner of Kitwancool Village*
● Lawren Harris's *Mt. Lefroy*
● J. E. H. MacDonald's *Forest Wilderness*
● A. Y. Jackson's *First Snow, Algoma*
● Tom Thomson's *Wood Interior, Winter*
● Arthur Lismer's *Bright Land*
● First Nations art

Museum of Contemporary Art

A new location, a (slightly) new name, and double the exhibition space are a testament to the success of the former Museum of Contemporary Canadian Art.

Striking regeneration The conversion of a heritage industrial building is a fitting location to display what the Minister of Canadian Heritage described as "Canada's unique perspective" to its best advantage. In addition to showing the museum's collection and staging exhibitions, the presence of more than 20 artists' and artisans' studios will promote the creation of exciting new works and bring a living and evolving element to the space.

An inclusive collection Founded in 1999, and opened on this site in May 2018, the museum

Artist's impression of the revitalised exterior (left); the striking Tower Automotive Building before its renovation (right)

is at the heart of the up-and-coming neighborhood of Junction Triangle in west Toronto, with its microbreweries, converted lofts and transportation links. Its new home is the former Tower Automotive Building, at 10 stories once the city's tallest building and still a landmark in this low-rise area. Here, on the lower two floors, the museum balances its national importance with a high level of inclusivity for the local community, with talks and workshops as well as major exhibitions. The permanent collection has more than 400 works by about 150 artists, including locals Stephen Andrews and Shelagh Keeley (who is known for her huge wall drawings) as well as figurative painter Ivan Eyre, and abstract artist Harold Klunder. In addition, there are works in other media, such as video installation, photography and performance.

THE BASICS

museumofcontemporaryart.ca

➕ See map ▷ 92
✉ 158 Sterling Road
☎ 416/395-0067
🌐 See website
🍴 Drake Commissary
Ⓜ Lansdown or Dundas West
🚌 506 Dundas streetcar
♿ Good
💲 Expensive

Ontario Science Centre

TOP
25

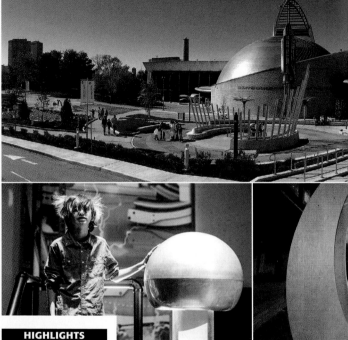

HIGHLIGHTS

● AstraZeneca Human Edge
● Science Arcade
● Living Earth
● Space Hall
● Cohon Family Nature Escape

TIPS

● Look for staff wearing lab coats—they are there to help and explain.
● You save money on combined tickets if you decide to see an IMAX movie.
● KidSpark
● Hot Zone

This leading interactive science museum, with its 10 exhibition spaces, designs and builds exhibits for others. It also has one of the few meteorites from Mars on public display in Canada.

Hands-on The Cohon Family Nature Escape is an outdoor area with interactive exhibits connecting science to nature and the landscape. The Planetarium offers shows about the cosmos, and the space exhibit delves deeper into discoveries about the universe. Designed with teens in mind, the Weston Family Innovation Centre provides "experiences" rather than exhibits, challenging young people to look at things differently and develop their skills, from making unusual music and art to learning how to read the body language of a liar. KidSpark

Indoor and outdoor interactive exhibits at Ontario Science Centre

provides similar fun for the under-8s, with water play, construction projects, musical experiences and other activities. In the AstraZeneca Human Edge, biology and physiology are explored.

Old favorites The Science Arcade is where you'll find the popular hair-raising electricity demonstration, the distorted room, pedal power, and puzzles and illusions. Living Earth has a recreated rain forest and other wonders, while in the Human Body hall you can see how you'll look as you age. The Sport hall combines athletic activities with virtual sport experiences.

Movie magic The Omnimax Theatre features a 24m (79ft) dome screen with digital wrap-around sound that, from the tilted seats, creates the illusion of being right in the movie.

THE BASICS

ontarioscience
centre.ca

✚ See map ▷ 92

✉ 770 Don Mills Road, North York at Eglinton

☎ 416/696-1000 or 1-888/696-1110

🕐 Sun–Fri 10–5, Sat 10–8

🍴 Restaurant, cafés

🚇 Pape then bus 25 or 185 Express north; Eglinton then bus 34 east

♿ Very good

✋ Expensive

Toronto Zoo

This polar bear and gorilla are among the 5,000 animals housed at the zoo

THE BASICS

torontozoo.com
🖶 See map ▷ 93
✉ 2000 Meadowvale Road
☎ 416/392-5929
🕐 May–Aug 9–7, Sep–Apr 9.30–4.30 (till 6pm on weekends and holidays from Sep–Nov)
🍴 Various outlets
🚇 Kennedy then Scarborough bus 86A going east (service varies in fall and winter)
♿ Very good
💵 Expensive (parking extra)
❓ "Meet the Keeper" program daily

HIGHLIGHTS

● Canadian Domain
● Giant pandas
● Tundra Trek
● Gorilla Rainforest
● Great Barrier Reef

TIP

● Admission is discounted during the low season, mid-Oct–Apr.

The 5,000 or so animals here, representing more than 450 species, occupy seven zoogeographical zones that recreate their natural environment as much as possible. The zoo is known for its conservation and successful breeding program.

Australasia, Eurasia and the Americas The 287ha (710 acres) are organized around pavilions and outdoor paddocks. Inside each pavilion, habitats and climates are replicated using flora, fauna, birds and butterflies. The Australasia Pavilion includes a 7m (23ft) long Great Barrier Reef tank, circular column tanks for jellyfish and other sea creatures, and an Outback area. The nearby Eurasia Outdoor Exhibit includes the Siberian tiger, snow leopard and yak. The Americas Pavilion includes alligators, black widow spiders, boa constrictors, Mojave desert sidewinders and pink-toed tarantulas. The Tundra Trek showcases polar bears, snowy owls, arctic foxes, and arctic wolves.

Africa and the Indo-Malayan Pavilion The Africa Pavilion houses the Gorilla Rainforest. Outdoors, you can observe zebra, lion, giraffe, ostrich, cheetah, hyena, white rhino and antelope. The orangutan and white-handed gibbon entertain in the Indo-Malaya Pavilion. Near the pavilion are the Sumatran tiger, Indian rhinoceros, lion-tailed macaque and, in the Malayan Woods Pavilion, clouded leopard. In the Canadian Domain is a large herd of wood bison plus grizzly bear, lynx and cougar.

More to See

AFRICAN LION SAFARI

lionsafari.com

More than 1,000 animals (not just lions) are kept in spacious drive-through reserves, including rhinos, primates, giraffes, zebras and elephants. There are boat and train rides, demonstrations and a jungle playground and wet play area.

➕ See map ▷ 93 ✉ 1386 Cooper Road, Hamilton. Take Hwy 401 to Hwy 6 south ☎ 519/623-2620 or 800/461-9453 🕐 May–Aug 10–5.30, Sep–Oct 10–4 🍴 Cafeteria/snack bar 💷 Expensive

AGA KHAN MUSEUM

agakhanmuseum.org

The beautiful modern building, flooded with natural light, houses exquisite examples of Islamic art, some dating back more than 1,200 years. Exhibits range from calligraphy and illustrations to paintings, ceramics and metalwork. Special exhibitions highlight particular periods or aspects of Islamic culture. The museum is within a lovely small park.

➕ See map ▷ 93 ✉ 77 Wynford Drive ☎ 416/646-4677 or 844/859-3671 🕐 Tue–Sun 10–6 (Wed until 8) 💷 Moderate (free Wed 4–8pm) 🎟 Guided tours at 11 and 3 (also 6pm Wed); park tour Tue–Sun at 4.15 🚇 Eglinton then bus 34AC east

THE BEACHES

At the eastern end of Queen Street, this district has a small-town atmosphere, with a boardwalk along the lake and attractive Victorian homes along tree-shaded streets. A variety of specialty stores, restaurants, cafés and antiques shops add interest. The largest of the neighborhood's four beaches is Woodbine Beach, its wide, sandy lakeshore backed by a pleasant green park.

➕ See map ▷ 93 🚋 Queen Street East streetcar

EDWARDS GARDENS

This botanical garden is popular in good weather, especially in early summer when the roses and rhododendrons are in flower.

Giraffes and zebras examine a visitor to the African Lion Safari

Playing volleyball at The Beaches

⊞ See map ▷ 92 ✉ 755 Lawrence Avenue East ☎ 416/392-8188 🕐 Daily dawn–dusk 🚇 Eglinton then Lawrence East bus 54, 54A ♿ Good 💲 Free

KORTRIGHT CENTRE FOR CONSERVATION

kortright.org

At this conservation and environmental facility, you can also enjoy more than 16km (10 miles) of hiking trails through forest and marshland.
⊞ See map ▷ 92 ✉ 9550 Pine Valley Drive, Woodbridge ☎ 905/832-2289 🕐 Daily 9.30–4 🍴 Café ♿ Good 💲 Inexpensive

SCARBOROUGH BLUFFS

Created by erosion, the dramatic Scarborough Bluffs line a 15km (9.3-mile) stretch of lakeshore to the east of Toronto, rising to more than 90m (295ft). One of the best spots to view the cliffs is from Bluffers Park, where there's a good beach, picnic areas, a restaurant and boat ramps.
⊞ See map ▷ 93

TODMORDEN MILLS

The old buildings of a mill, established in the late 18th century, tell the story of Toronto's early industrial history. You can explore the former homes of the millers and see the old Don train station, the Brewery Gallery and the Papermill Theatre and Gallery. A path leads to a wildflower preserve.
⊞ See map ▷ 92 ✉ 67 Pottery Road ☎ 416/396-2819 🕐 Jun–Aug Tue–Fri 10–4.30, Sat–Sun 12–5, rest of year Wed–Fri 12–4, Sat–Sun 12–4.30 🚇 Broadview, then northbound buses to Mortimer Avenue ♿ Few 💲 Inexpensive

TOMMY THOMPSON PARK

On an artificial spit of land that curves out into the lake, this area has been colonized by muskrats, woodchucks, foxes, coyotes, snakes, turtles and toads and around 45 bird species.
⊞ See map ▷ 92 ✉ Off south end of Leslie Street ☎ 416/661-6600 🕐 Apr–Oct Sat–Sun 9–6; Nov–Mar Sat–Sun 9–4.30 🚍 97B ♿ Good 💲 Free

Bluffers Park Marina at the base of Scarborough Bluffs

Excursions

KLEINBURG

Picturesque Kleinburg, on a wooded ridge above the Humber River, is a 19th-century heritage town full of lovely restored homes, specialty stores, spas, restaurants and galleries. The Kleinburg Nashville Historical Collection, open on summer weekends, displays artifacts and photographs of the town. It's also a good base to explore the Humber River trails, on foot or on bikes. The big event of the year is the annual Binder Twine Festival, dating back to the days when farmers would come to town at harvest time to buy twine for their sheaves. It still has an old-time feel, with traditional crafts and entertainment, and the highlight is the choosing of the Binder Twine Queen. The McMichael Canadian Art Collection is also in Kleinburg (▷ 97).

MIDLAND

On the southern shore of beautiful Georgian Bay, this summer vacation hub clusters around the harbor. A short downtown tour reveals 34 huge historic murals on the walls of business premises. The most remarkable, 60m (200ft) across by 25m (80ft) high, covers a grain elevator on the harborfront.

Midland is also home to the only Canadian national shrine outside Quebec, the Martyrs' Shrine, commemorating eight Jesuit missionaries who lived among the local Huron tribe for 10 years until they were slaughtered by the Iroquois. The fortified mission, Sainte-Marie Among the Hurons, has been recreated on its original site opposite the shrine. Contained within a wooden palisade, it includes a church, homes, workshops and barracks, all brought to life by costumed staff. On the edge of Little Lake, the Huronia Museum has a reconstructed typical Huron village. From the European settlement there are military artifacts, furniture and art collections. Other attractions include the Wye Marsh Wildlife Centre and sightseeing cruises around the thousands of islands in Georgian Bay.

THE BASICS

kleinburgvillage.ca
🚆 GO train from Union station to Malton, then Bolton bus

THE BASICS

midland.ca
✉ 527 Len Self Boulevard
☎ 705/526-7884
Martyrs' Shrine
martyrs-shrine.com
✉ 16163 Highway 12 East ☎ 705/526-4770, ext 3206 🕐 May–Oct daily 8am–9pm
👣 Inexpensive
Sainte-Marie Among the Hurons
saintemarieamong thehurons.on.ca
✉ 16164 Highway 12 East ☎ 705/526-7838
🕐 May–early Oct daily 10–5 👣 Moderate (inexpensive out of season)
Huronia Museum
huroniamuseum.com
✉ 549 Little Lake Park Road ☎ 705/526-2844
🕐 Daily 9–5 mid-May–mid-Oct, Mon–Fri 9–5, rest of year 👣 Moderate

NIAGARA FALLS

This natural wonder of the world is on most visitors' itineraries. The Canadian side of the falls gives a far superior view to the American and though the town is marred by kitschy commercial outlets, nothing can detract from the breathtaking sight of the falls.

Thundering water The best way to appreciate the power of the falls is to stand at the very top, on Table Rock, at the point where a dark green mass of water silently slithers into the abyss. It is totally mesmerizing, if rather wet. When you can tear yourself away, descend about 45m (150ft) by elevator to the two outdoor observation decks directly behind the falls. Here, more than anywhere, you can appreciate the tremendous power of the falling water.

Get up close Don't miss the Hornblower Niagara Cruises boat ride, which departs from the bottom of Clifton Hill. You board in calm waters (and don the waterproofs provided), then voyage right into the horseshoe and the turmoil of water at the foot of the falls, venturing just a little bit farther than seems sensible. Soaked by the incredible spray (but protected by plastic ponchos), you can look up at the huge wall of water plummeting down on three sides—Niagara means "thundering water."

Making a day of it A little way downstream, a bend in the river forms a huge whirlpool, and you can view it from above by riding the historic Whirlpool Aero Car or from below on one of the thrilling jet-boat rides. There is also the White Water Walk, a boardwalk right at the edge of the rapids. About 8km (5 miles) north along the Niagara Parkway is the Niagara Parks Botanical Gardens, which includes a butterfly conservatory. The 56km (35-mile) Niagara Parkway winds along the Niagara River from Chippawa to Niagara-on-the-Lake past orchards, wineries, parks and picnic areas—it's a joy for scenic biking and hiking.

THE BASICS

niagarafallstourism.com
Distance: 130km (81 miles)
Journey Time: 1 hour 30 mins
🚌 Public Transit Greyhound
🚉 GO Transit summer weekends
☎ 416/594-1311
🛈 5400 Robinson Street
☎ 905/356-6061 or 800/563-2557

The Niagara Parks Commission

niagaraparks.com
✉ Welcome centers: Table Rock Centre; Murray Hill; Clifton Hill at Falls Avenue; Grand View Marketplace outside Hornblower Niagara Cruises ticket booth; Rapidsview
☎ 905/356-2241 or 877/642-7275

Toronto's accommodations range from budget hotels and modest bed-and-breakfasts to temples of luxury. Wherever you stay, the renowned Canadian welcome is going to make a lasting impression.

Where to Stay

Introduction

Toronto has some of the finest and most innovative hotels in the world, and staying downtown can be more picturesque than in many other cities. Here, the modern high-rise hotels might have spectacular views over the lake, while modest, more economical bed-and-breakfasts will probably be in superbly restored heritage homes on leafy residential streets surprisingly close to the center, and conveniently located for all the major sights in the city.

Be prepared

The city has more than 43,000 hotel rooms to suit a range of tastes and budgets, and it is might be surprising to learn that it is possible to just show up in the city and find a room—even, perhaps, a last-minute deal on the price. That said, it's usually better to arrive with a reservation. The city can fill up when a major festival is on, and advance online prices are often a lot lower than for walk-ins. If you do show up without a reservation, try the Travellers' Aid Society of Toronto (travellersaid.ca). This helpful service can found at a booth in Union Station (tel 416/366-7788), and is open daily 9.30–9.30.

Hidden costs

Be aware that quoted room rates may not always include local taxes: 13 percent HST and possibly an additional 4 percent municipal tax, currently under consideration. If you arrive by car, some downtown hotels with parking garages will charge a daily parking fee while others may charge for valet parking, which can prove quite costly so check costs in advance of your arrival.

HOME AWAY FROM HOME

If you are a family or group and staying for a week or more, it might be worth looking for a vacation rental—even couples can save money this way. Using the properties to full capacity, you could get a per person nightly rate of as little as $40 and make further savings by cooking for yourselves. Try visiting vrbo.com or airbnb.com.

Budget Hotels

PRICES
Expect to pay under $200 per night for a double room in a budget hotel.

ALEXANDRA HOTEL
alexandrahotel.com
Convenient for Downtown West attractions, this modern block has simple, comfortable rooms with kitchenettes.
➕ H6 ✉ 77 Ryerson Avenue ☎ 416/504-9195 or 800/567-1893 🚊 501 streetcar to Augusta Avenue

DELTA TORONTO EAST
deltahotels.com
Attractive and modern, this hotel in Scarborough has a large pool with waterslides, saunas and a fitness room, plus a supervised kids' center.
➕ Off map to east ✉ 2035 Kennedy Road, Scarborough ☎ 416/299-1500 or 1-800/663-3386 🚊 Kennedy, then bus 43

DOWNTOWN HOME INN
downtownhomeinn.com
Modern rooms have hardwood floors, air-conditioning and WiFi (but bring your own soap). Near Royal Ontario Museum and Yorkville, it's hospitable and friendly and the price incudes breakfast.
➕ M3 ✉ 2 Monteith Street ☎ 647/342-1010 🚊 Wellesley

HOWARD JOHNSON'S INN, YORKVILLE
hojo.com
In a great location, this hotel offers friendly and obliging service and is good value, with spacious, modern rooms. The price includes breakfast, WiFi and use of the gym. There's also on-site parking (for a fee).
➕ L1 ✉ 89 Avenue Road ☎ 416/964-1220 🚊 Bay or St. George

ISABELLA HOTEL & SUITES
isabellahotel.com
A historic and visual landmark, this hotel consists of an 1891 mansion and a 1914 seven-story tower, renovated and transformed into a boutique hotel.
➕ N2 ✉ 556 Sherbourne Street ☎ 416/922-2203 🚊 Bloor/Yonge or Wellesley

MADISON MANOR BOUTIQUE HOTEL
madisonmanorboutiquehotel.com
This Victorian home is well placed for Bloor-Yorkville and the Royal Ontario Museum. It has traditional furnishings, some of the 23 bedrooms have fireplaces and a few have a balcony.
➕ J1 ✉ 20 Madison Avenue ☎ 416/922-5579 or 1-877/561-7048 🚊 Spadina or St. George

VICTORIA'S MANSION GUEST HOUSE
victoriasmansion.com
In a peaceful location near Bloor-Yorkville, this lovely historic home fronted by a nice garden preserves many historic features but provides modern amenities (air-conditioning, WiFi, refrigerator, microwave). Breakfast is not served but there are plenty of options nearby.
➕ M3 ✉ 68 Gloucester Street ☎ 416/921-4625 🚊 Wellesley

WESTIN PRINCE
westinprincetoronto.com
Serenely set in 6ha (15 acres), just 20 minutes from downtown in the Don Valley. Its Katsura restaurant has excellent Japanese cuisine. The hotel also has a fitness center.
➕ Off map to northeast ✉ 900 York Mills Road, Don Mills ☎ 416/444-2511 🚊 York Mills

Mid-Range Hotels

BOND PLACE

bondplace.ca

Just steps from Yonge-Dundas Square, the Eaton Centre and theaters, this hotel has light and attractive modern rooms and suites. Health-conscious guests will appreciate the fitness room, Mediterranean cuisine and juice bar. It has inexpensive on-site parking.

➕ M5 ✉ 65 Dundas Street East ☎ 416/362-6061 or 1-800/268-9390 🚇 Dundas

THE DRAKE HOTEL

thedrakehotel.ca

Stylish, a bit quirky and with a loyal clientele who swear they wouldn't stay anywhere else, this hotel has a range of room styles and an interesting program of entertainment and art events.

➕ D6 ✉ 1150 Queen Street West ☎ 416/531-5042 🚋 501 Queen streetcar

EATON CHELSEA

eatonhotels.com

Large (1,590 rooms) but well run, the Chelsea has good-sized rooms, some with great downtown views (if you like skyscrapers). Its excellent facilities for children include a swimming pool, play room and an area for teens.

➕ M4 ✉ 33 Gerrard Street West ☎ 416/595-1975 or 1-800/243-5732 🚇 College

HILTON GARDEN INN TORONTO DOWNTOWN

hiltongardeninn3.hilton.com

At the lower end of this price bracket, this is an all-suite hotel with buffet breakfast included, and the indoor pool and downtown location between Queen Street West and the Entertainment District makes it a good choice.

➕ N5 ✉ 92 Peter Street ☎ 855/618-4697 🚋 504 King Street streetcar

HOLIDAY INN BLOOR YORKVILLE

ihg.com

It's a modern hotel, with fairly standard Holiday Inn rooms, but it is in a good spot for visiting Yorkville and the Royal Ontario Museum.

➕ J2 ✉ 280 Bloor Street West ☎ 416/968-0010 or 0800/911-617 🚇 St. George

HOTEL LE GERMAIN

germaintoronto.com

This is part of a small, stylish and modern Montréal chain. A fireplace warms the minimalist lobby-lounge and top-quality linens, toiletries and Bose stereo systems set the scene in the rooms. Flexible checkout times are a bonus.

➕ J/K7 ✉ 30 Mercer Street ☎ 416/345-9500 🚇 Union

HOTEL OCHO

hotelocho.com

In between Chinatown and the Fashion District, this hotel has a pleasing austere decor of wood, brick and local art. Bathrooms are all marble and granite. It's a popular wedding venue.

➕ J6 ✉ 195 Spadina Avenue ☎ 416/593-0885 🚇 Mimico 🚋 510 Spadina streetcar

HOTEL VICTORIA

hotelvictoria-toronto.com

In an older building in the financial district, this boutique hotel retains many original features in public areas and has 56 rooms with hardwood floors, pillow-top beds and sleek bathrooms.

🛨 M7 ✉ 56 Yonge Street ☎ 416/363-1666 or 1-800/363-8228 🚇 King

MAKING WAVES BOATEL

boatel.ca

A unique B&B on an elegant converted trawler in a prime location on the downtown waterfront. It has state rooms, lounge, a galley kitchen and covered deck. Comfortable rooms have stunning views. It's open June to September only.

🛨 D9 ✉ 539 Queens Quay West ☎ 647/403-2764 🚇 Exhibition

MARRIOTT CITY CENTRE

marriott.com

Out of 348 functional rooms, 70 overlook the Rogers Centre baseball turf. Pool, fitness center and squash courts.

🛨 J8 ✉ 1 Blue Jays Way ☎ 416/341-7100 or 1-866/237-1512 🚇 Union

MARRIOTT EATON CENTRE

marriott.com

Perfectly located for shopping (the Eaton Centre is next door), restaurants, and Yonge-Dundas Square, this hotel has high-tech amenities, restaurants, lounges and a pool on the top floor.

🛨 L5 ✉ 525 Bay Street ☎ 416/597-9200 or 1-800/905-0667 🚇 Dundas

OLD MILL TORONTO

oldmilltoronto.com

If modern high-rise city-center hotels don't appeal, this refined alternative is away from the city bustle but near a subway station. The romantic Tudor-style building has elegant traditional-style rooms and suites. There's an on-site spa and a bar with live jazz.

🛨 Off map to north ✉ 21 Old Mill Road ☎ 416/236-2641 or 1-866/653-6455 🚇 Old Mill

OMNI KING EDWARD

omnihotels.com

This architectural jewel in marble and sculpted stucco has spacious rooms and suites that are nicely decorated and well equipped.

🛨 M7 ✉ 37 King Street East ☎ 416/863-9700 🚇 King

RADISSON PLAZA HOTEL ADMIRAL

radisson.com

On the harborfront, this hotel has a rooftop pool, bar and terrace. The 157 rooms are well furnished and equipped.

🛨 K9 ✉ 249 Queens Quay West ☎ 416/203-3333 or 1-800/201-1718 🚇 Union

THE SOHO METROPOLITAN HOTEL

metropolitan.com

Expect sophisticated, tech-savy rooms with luxurious bathrooms and dressing rooms. The contemporary luxe style continues to the Dale Chihuly artwork and the top-class Luckee Restaurant serving gourmet Chinese cuisine.

🛨 J7 ✉ 318 Wellington Street West ☎ 416/599-8800 🚇 Union

STRATHCONA

thestrathconahotel.com

Some rooms may be small but the location is good, and you'll pay less than at the Royal York across the street.

🛨 L7 ✉ 60 York Street ☎ 416/363-3321 🚇 Union

Luxury Hotels

DOUBLETREE

hilton.com

Just behind City Hall and Nathan Phillips Square, this slick and stylish hotel has two restaurants, a gym and an indoor pool. Rooms and suites are light and spacious and all are nonsmoking.

✚ L5 ✉ 108 Chestnut Street ☎ 416/977-5000 Ⓢ St. Patrick

FAIRMONT ROYAL YORK

fairmont.com

This iconic hotel is the grande-dame of Toronto accommodations, blending historic charm and friendly service. Millions have been spent on renovating rooms and amenities. It features nine bars and restaurants—the Library Bar is noted for its martinis. It has a pool.

✚ L7 ✉ 100 Front Street West ☎ 416/368-2511 or 1/800-257-7544 (reservations only) Ⓢ Union

FOUR SEASONS

fourseasons.com

In the heart of Yorkville, this is the city's top hotel. The service is personal yet unobtrusive, the rooms are spacious, elegant, comfortable and well equipped, and the facilities excellent. It has a great bar, DBar (▷ 88), and the fashionable Café Boulud attracts a celebrity crowd.

✚ L1 ✉ 60 Yorkville Avenue ☎ 416/964-0411 Ⓢ Bay

HOTEL X

hotelxtoronto.com

There are stunning views at this new 30-story resort at Exhibition Place. In addition to more than 400 luxurious rooms and suites, there's fine dining at Petros 82, a three-story bar overlooking the lake, a rooftop pool, movie theaters, sport and fitness amenities and event spaces. For younger guests there's a huge play center and babysitting services.

✚ E8 ✉ 111 Princes' Boulevard, Exhibition Place ☎ 416/943-9300 Ⓡ Exhibition

ONE KING WEST

onekingwest.com

Luxurious accommodations in the heart of downtown range from good-sized studios to the stunning Panorama Suite with, as the name suggests, a far-reaching view. Teller's Bar and Lounge in the lobby occupies the former bank.

✚ B7 ✉ 1 King Street West ☎ 416/548-8100 or 1-866/470-5464 Ⓢ King

SUITES AT 1 KING WEST

onekingwest.com

Stunning contemporary suites and a health club in a landmark high-rise hotel near many top attractions. It incorporates the historic former hall of the Toronto Dominion Bank.

✚ M7 ✉ 1 King Street West ☎ 416/548-8100 Ⓢ King 🚋 504 King streetcar

WESTIN HARBOUR CASTLE

westinharbourcastletoronto.com

Handy for many sights, including the CN Tower, Scotiabank Arena, and the Entertainment and Financial districts, this large, 38-story hotel is in a fabulous lakefront location. Many of the 977 rooms have a lake view, and all are well appointed and comfortable. Excellent amenities include Toula, for fine Italian dining, squash and tennis courts, and an indoor pool, making for a pleasant stay.

✚ M9 ✉ 1 Harbour Square ☎ 416/869-1600 Ⓢ Union

Here is the key information to smooth your path both before you go and when you arrive. Get savvy with the local transportation, explore Toronto or check out what festivals are taking place.

Planning Ahead

When to Go

The best time to visit Toronto is in summer, when Canada's Wonderland and all the other attractions are open, and the ferries to the islands are in full swing. Fall is also good. The weather is still warm, and outside the city the forests take on a rich golden glow.

TIME

Toronto is on Eastern Standard Time, three hours ahead of Los Angeles, and five hours behind GMT.

AVERAGE DAILY MAXIMUM TEMPERATURES

JAN	FEB	MAR	APR	MAY	JUN	JUL	AUG	SEP	OCT	NOV	DEC
25°F	26°F	35°F	47°F	57°F	66°F	70°F	70°F	64°F	53°F	42°F	30°F
−4°C	−3°C	1°C	8°C	14°C	19°C	21°C	21°C	18°C	12°C	6°C	−1°C

Spring (mid-March to late May) is unpredictable. Occasional snow or ice storms occur as late as mid-April.
Summer (early June to late August) is warm to hot, with occasional rain or humidity and cooler evenings.
Fall (September and October) has cooler temperatures, sunny days and occasional rain; the weather is ideal for exploring.
Winter (November to March) can be harsh. November is always unpredictable and mid-winter is much colder because of the unrelenting winds blowing off Lake Ontario.

SPORTING CALENDAR

Athletics
Toronto Waterfront Marathon: Oct
Toronto Marathon: May
Baseball
Toronto Blue Jays, Rogers Centre: Apr–Oct
Basketball
Toronto Raptors, Scotiabank Arena: Oct–Apr
Football
Toronto Argonauts, BMO Field: Jun–Oct
Championship games: Grey Cup (national), Vanier Cup (university) and Metro Bowl (high school): all late Nov

Hockey
Toronto Maple Leafs, Scotiabank Arena: Oct–Apr
Toronto Marlies, Ricoh Coliseum, Exhibition Place: Oct–Apr
Horse racing
Queen's Plate Woodbine Racetrack: late Jun/early Jul
Lacrosse
Toronto Rock, Scotiabank Arena: Jan–May
Motor Racing
Honda Indy Toronto, Exhibition Place: Jul

Soccer
Toronto Lynx and Lady Lynx, Centennial Park Stadium, Etobicoke: May–Jul
Toronto FC, BMO Field: Apr–Oct
Water sports
Dragon Boat Race Festival, Toronto Islands: mid-Jun
Great White North International Dragon Boat Race, Western Beaches Watercourse, Marilyn Bell Park: early Sep

Toronto Online

seetorontonow.com
Toronto's official tourist website is run by
the Toronto Convention and Visitors Association.
It contains details of shopping, accommodations, attractions, theaters and restaurants.

toronto.com
A comprehensive Toronto guide with good
event and concert listings, shopping information, plus excellent links to other useful sites.

web.toronto.ca
The City of Toronto's comprehensive attractions
guide, with history and archive photos.

where.ca/toronto
Practical info and up-to-date event listings.

thestar.com and torontolife.com
Two good media sites with listings.

ontariotravel.net
Ontario's official travel information site.

niagarafallstourism.com
Niagara Tourism's official site.

niagaraparks.com
Niagara region tourist information, focusing on
events and attractions.

tapa.ca
Toronto Alliance for the Performing Arts site
listing all the theater, dance, opera, comedy and
musical theater companies in Toronto; links to
box offices and ticket agencies.

ttc.ca
Toronto Transit Commission site, with details
about buses, subways and streetcars.

activeto.ca
Information and maps for walking, hiking,
cycling and activities in and around Toronto.

TRAVEL SITES

fodors.com
A complete travel-planning
site. Reserve air tickets, cars
and rooms; research prices
and weather; pose ques-
tions to fellow travelers;
and find links to other sites.

worldweb.com
A comprehensive travel
guide. Plan your trip aided
by online hotel reservation,
info about transportation,
weather, restaurants,
events and shopping. Maps
and photo gallery.

WIFI IN THE CITY

**Toronto Reference
Library** is the best place to
go online if you don't have
your own device. The banks
of computers can be used
for long or short periods.
✉ 789 Yonge Street
☎ 416/395-5577
🕐 Mon–Fri 9–8.30
📶 Free

Wireless Toronto provides
information about free
WiFi hotspots throughout
Toronto at wirelesstoronto.
ca. Free WiFi is also available through the City of
Toronto at City Hall, at
all TTC stations and at
the Pearson International
Airport. Many restaurants,
including Tim Hortons,
offer free WiFi.

Getting There

ENTRY REQUIREMENTS

Citizens of EU and most British Commonwealth countries require a valid passport and a return or onward ticket but no visa. US citizens returning from abroad (including Canada) by land, sea or air need to show a valid passport or other documents. People under 18 must have a parent or guardian letter stating a length of stay. If children are traveling with a divorced parent who shares custody, that parent must carry the legal custody documents. If children are traveling with adults who are not parents or guardians, those adults must carry the written permission of the parents or guardians.

Visitors from certain countries who are flying into Canada (but not entering by land or sea) need to obtain an Electronic Travel Authorization, to be presented with their passport at check-in. This includes British citizens and legal permanent residents of the US; the latter also need to show their Green Card. For a list of the countries concerned, visit: cic.gc.ca/english/visit/visas-all.asp For visa requirements, visit: cic.gc.ca/english/visit/apply-who.asp.

AIRPORT

Pearson International Airport lies northwest of Toronto, about 22.5km (14 miles) from the city center. Billy Bishop Toronto City Airport is located on the Toronto Islands, just south of Downtown.

ARRIVING BY AIR

Taxis and limos leave from the arrivals level of all terminals of Pearson International Airport (tel 416/247-7678). Fare is determined by zone; arrange in advance with dispatcher or driver. Downtown: Expect to pay $50–$60; journey time 30–40 mins.

Airport Rocket (bus 192) departs daily 5.30am–2am to Kipling Station, Dundas Street and East Mall Crescent; journey time 20 mins. Passengers arriving at night can take 300A Bloor-Danforth route (45 mins) to Yonge and Bloor; or 307 to Bathurst. Both night services run half-hourly. Ticket price is $3.25 (one-way). Contact Toronto Transit Commission (TTC tel 416/393-4636; ttc.ca).

GO Transit has an hourly bus to Yorkdale and Finch bus terminals (Terminal 1); Mon–Sat 6am–1am, Sun 9am–1am; journey time 30 mins to Yorkdale and 45 mins to York Mills (tel 416/869-3200; gotransit.com).

Union Pearson Express (UP Express) airport rail link service runs between Union Station (Downtown) and Pearson Airport (Terminal 1), with stops at Bloor and Weston GO Stations.

Travel time is 25 minutes, with daily departures every 15 minutes from 5.30am to 1am.

Billy Bishop Toronto City Airport (tel 416/ 203-6492; portstoronto.com) is mainly used by regional airlines, such as Porter Airlines (flyporter.com), which flies to various major cities in Eastern Canada and the USA. The ferry to and from the airport docks every 15 mins, daily 5.15am–midnight and takes 90 seconds. Free for pedestrians and $11 for vehicles (round trip). A pedestrian tunnel provides additional access to the airport. The entrance is beside the ferry terminal, and, with moving walkways and escalators, it takes about six minutes to reach the airport.

ARRIVING BY BUS
Greyhound Canada (tel 416/594-1010; 800/661-8747) goes to Toronto Coach Terminal (tel 416/971-9452) at 610 Bay Street. Dundas and St. Patrick subway stations are nearby.

ARRIVING BY CAR
From Michigan, you enter Detroit-Windsor via I-75 and the Ambassador Bridge or Port Huron-Sarnia via I-94 and the Bluewater Bridge. From New York State, using I-90 you enter at Buffalo-Fort Erie; Niagara Falls, NY–Niagara Falls; or Niagara Falls, NY–Lewiston. Using I-81, you can cross at Hill Island; using Route 37, you cross either at Ogdensburg–Johnstown or Rooseveltown–Cornwall. Once across the border, you approach Toronto from the west by Queen Elizabeth Way or Highway 401, from the east by Highway 2 or Highway 401. Boston is 896km (557 miles) from Toronto; Buffalo 169km (105 miles); Chicago 838km (521 miles); New York 801km (498 miles).

ARRIVING BY TRAIN
Amtrak (tel 800/872-7245 in the US) and VIA Rail (tel 888/842-7245; viarail.ca in Canada) long-distance trains arrive at Union Station, which is linked directly to the subway.

NEED TO KNOW GETTING THERE

Getting Around

Toronto has an excellent and reliable public transportation network, comprising subway, buses and streetcars.

DRIVING IN TORONTO

The city speed limit is 31mph (50kph), and right turns at red lights are permitted unless posted otherwise, but pedestrians on crosswalks have priority. Seat belts are compulsory. Towing is among the parking penalties. Call Trip Info (☎ 416/599-9090) for details of road closures.

VISITORS WITH A DISABILITY

Currently 35 subway stations are accessible, with more planned. The TTC's bus fleet is wheelchair and scooter friendly, as are all bus routes and, soon, streetcars. Visit the TTC website (ttc.ca). Wheel-Trans offers a door-to-door service (5am–11pm) for registered customers (☎ 416/ 393-4111, 416/393-4311 for hearing impaired). Parking privileges are extended to drivers who have disabled plates or a pass allowing parking in "No Parking" zones. Many buildings are barrier-free and well equipped with elevators. For more information, contact Toronto Community Foundation ✉ 33 Bloor Street East, Suite 1603, Toronto, ON M4W 3H1 ☎ 416/921-2035 ⊘ Daily

SUBWAY, STREETCARS AND BUSES

● The subway is fast and easy to use.
● The subway consists of four major lines, Yonge–University–Spadina (1), Bloor–Danforth (2), Scarborough RT (3), and Sheppard (4). Line 1 has 38 stations and runs South from Finch to Union Station in downtown Toronto then up to Sheppard West, where it turns west to Vaughan. Line 2 has 31 stations and runs from east to west along Bloor Street and Danforth Avenue. Line 3 is a rapid transit route with six stations, linking the eastern end of Line 2 with Scarborough and Line 4 runs east to west along Sheppard Avenue East.
● You need a token ($3.25 for a single fare; adults can save by buying 3 tokens for $9; students and senior citizens can save even more by buying 5 tokens for $10.25), which can be bought in any subway station. Drop it into the box at the ticket window or into the turnstile. Day, weekly and monthly passes are available. A day pass ($12.50) covers one adult from the start of service until 5.30am the next day, for unlimited travel on all regular TTC routes. On weekends and statutory holidays, the same ticket will cover a family: either two adults, or two adults and up to four children aged 19 or under, or one adult and up to five children aged 19 or under. The weekly pass costs $43.75 ($34.75 for students and senior citizens); the monthly Metropass costs $146.25 ($116.75 for students and senior citizens).
● Discounts are available for students aged 13 to 19, and senior citizens aged 65 and over. Children under 12 travel free.
● The subway system is connected to the bus and streetcar network. It is always wise to pick up a transfer at the subway station from the red push-button machine at the entrance or from the bus driver. By so doing, you can board a streetcar going east or west from the subway

station if you need to, or transfer from the bus to the subway without paying extra. Transfers are only available for continuation of a journey, and can't be used if you stop over in between.

● If you are not transferring, a bus ride costs a token, or you can pay with the exact change.

● Bus stops are at or near corners and are marked by elongated signs with red stripes and bus and streetcar diagrams. Pick up a Ride Guide map at subway stations.

● Be warned—bus stops are not always easy to see.

● The subway operates Mon–Fri 6am–1.30am and Sun 9am–1.30am. A Blue Night Network is in operation outside those hours on basic surface routes, running about every 30 minutes. Blue reflective bands indicate the bus stops served.

● For transit information pick up a Ride Guide, available at subway stations, tourist offices and other public places, or call 416/393-4636 (7am–10pm).

TAXIS

● Cabs can be hailed on the street.

● The light on the rooftop will be turned on if the taxi is available.

● All taxis must display rates and contain a meter.

● Tip 15–20 percent.

● If you need to call for a cab, these are some of the options:
Beck Taxi tel 416/751-5555
City Taxi tel 416/740-2222
Co-op Cabs tel 416/504-2667
Crown Taxi tel 416/240-0000
Diamond Taxi tel 416/366-6868

● Water taxis offer rides to the Toronto Islands and some can be chartered by the hour.

DRIVING

You need your driver's license, car registration and proof of car insurance to drive in Canada. Check the latest information on travel documentation before leaving home.

VISITOR INFORMATION

You can obtain information from: Tourism Toronto ✉ Union Station on Front Street ☎ 416/392-9300 or 800/499-2514; seetorontonow.com ◷ Mon–Fri 8–5.

WOMEN ALONE

Anyone traveling alone on buses at night (9pm–5am) can request to get off between stops to be closer to their destination. If you require this service, let the driver know at least one stop before you want to get off. You will get off at the front, and rear bus doors are kept closed to prevent a fellow passenger from following.

Essential Facts

NATIONAL HOLIDAYS

New Year's Day
(January 1)
Family Day (third Monday
in February)
**Good Friday and/or
Easter Monday**
Victoria Day (Monday
before May 25)
Canada Day (July 1)
Civic Holiday (first Monday
in August; optional)
Labour Day (first Monday
in September)
Thanksgiving (second
Monday in October)
Remembrance Day
(November 11)
Christmas Day
(December 25)
Boxing Day (December 26)

MONEY

The Canadian dollar is the
unit of currency (= 100
cents). Coins include 10¢
(dime) and 25¢ (quarter),
and $1 (loonie) and $2
(twoonie). Bills are $5, $10,
$20, $50 and $100. Stores
may refuse large bills.
1 cent coins have been
phased out, making the
smallest denomination
5 cents. Whe paying in
cash, change is rounded up
or down accordingly.

ELECTRICITY
● 110v, 60Hz AC. US-style flat 2-pin plugs.

MEDICAL AND DENTAL TREATMENT
● 24-hour emergency service is provided by
the Toronto General Hospital, tel 416/340-
3111. The main entrance is at 200 Elizabeth
Street; other entrances are at 150 Gerrard
Street West and University Avenue, just south of
College Street.
● If you need a doctor, ask at your hotel or seek
a referral from the College of Physicians and
Surgeons at 80 College Street, tel 16/967-
2603, open 9–5.
● In a dental emergency, contact the Ontario
Dental Association, tel 416/922-3900.

MEDICINES
● Always bring a prescription for any medica-
tions in case of loss and also to show to the
customs officers if necessary.
● Shopper's Drug Mart (465 Yonge Street, tel
416/408-4000) stays open 24 hours. Rexall
Pharma Plus (63 Wellesley Street at Church,
tel 416/924-7760) is open until midnight.

MONEY MATTERS
● Most banks have ATMs linked to Cirrus, Plus
or other networks and this is the easiest way to
secure cash. Check your PIN is valid in Canada.
Also check on frequency and amount limits of
withdrawals. For ATM locations visit mastercard.
com for MasterCard and for Visa/Plus, visa.com.
● Credit cards are widely accepted. American
Express, Diner's Club, Discover, MasterCard
and Visa are the most common.
● Traveler's checks are accepted in all but small
shops as long as the denominations are low
($20 or $50). If you carry traveler's checks in
Canadian dollars, you save on conversion fees.

OPENING HOURS
● Banks: Mon–Fri 9 or 9.30–4 or 5; some are
open longer and some open Sat–Sun with
reduced hours.

- Museums: hours vary.
- Shops: generally Mon–Wed 9.30 or 10–6, Sat, Sun 10–5. Hours are often extended on Thu or Fri until 8 or 9. Malls stay open later than smaller stores.

POST OFFICES
- Postal services can be found at convenience and drugstores. Look for a sign in the window advertising postal services.
- There are also post office windows open in major shopping complexes such as Atrium on Bay (tel 416/506-0911); Commerce Court (tel 416/956-7452); Toronto Dominion Centre (tel 416/360-7105); First Canadian Place (tel 416/364-0540).

SMOKING
- Smoking is banned in all public buildings, except in clearly designated smoking areas. All bars and restaurants are nonsmoking zones. Usually, the ban also includes vaping.

TAXES
- The provincial harmonized sales tax (HST) is 13 percent. This applies to most items including retail, accommodations, and food.
- There are some exceptions to the HST that are only subjected to a 5 percent tax such as books, some baby items, newspapers, etc.

TELEPHONES
- To dial outside the Toronto area codes of 416, 647, 437, or 905 add the prefix 1.
- Avoid using phones in hotel rooms, which incur high charges, although some hotels offer free local calls.
- For long distance use AT&T, Bell or Sprint rather than calling direct. Access codes and instructions are found on your phone card. If they don't work, dial the operator and ask for the access code in Canada.
- To call the UK from Toronto dial 01144 and drop the first 0 from the number. To call the US from Toronto dial 1 plus the area code.

TIPPING

As a rule, tip around 15 percent in restaurants and bars, 15–20 percent to cab drivers, $1 per bag to porters and $1 to a valet parking attendant. Hairdressers also expect 15–20 percent. Tips are calculated on the pretax amount.

EMERGENCY NUMBERS

Fire, police, ambulance
☎ 911
Toronto Police Headquarters
✉ 40 College Street
☎ 416/808-2222
Rape Crisis
☎ 416/597-8808
Victim Services
☎ 416/808-7066
Lost property: For articles left on a bus, streetcar or subway, TTC Lost Articles Office ✉ Bay subway station ☎ 416/393-4100
🕐 Mon–Fri 8–5.
Consulates:
UK ✉ 777 Bay Street, Suite 2800 ☎ 416/593-1290
USA ☎ 360 University Avenue ☎ 416/595-1700 or, for visas, 437/887-1448
Portugal ✉ 438 University Avenue, Suite 1400, Box 41 ☎ 416/217-0966
Spain ✉ 2 Bloor Street East, Suite 1201 ☎ 416/977-1661

NEED TO KNOW ESSENTIAL FACTS

Festivals and Events

FILM FESTIVALS

Toronto and the movies are inseparable, with "Hollywood North" attracting the biggest names to the city's studios and locations. A clutch of festivals showcases new releases and recognizes the artistic contribution of those who made and starred in them. The Toronto International Film Festival (TIFF) in September is one of the most important film festivals in the world and the city is full of celebrities. TIFF Kids International Film Festival in March shows intelligent movies for kids, and other festivals include the Hot Docs Canadian International Documentary Festival (late April/early May); the Toronto Jewish Film Festival (May); the Toronto Inside Out LGBT Film Festival (late May–early June) and the Italian Contemporary Film Festival (June).

JANUARY/FEBRUARY

Winterlicious More than 200 city restaurants celebrate international cuisine with good-value fixed-price menus. *Late Jan/early Feb.*

MARCH

St. Patrick's Day One of the largest parades in the world starts at noon on Bloor Street (at St. George). *Nearest Sun to Mar 17.*
Canada Blooms & National Home Show The Direct Energy Centre at Exhibition Place hosts a showcase of homes and interiors. *Mar*.

MAY

Canadian Music Week For four days hundreds of bands play venues all over the city. Also a music industry conference, trade show and awards gala events. *Early May.*
Doors Open Toronto Around 150 historically and architecturally interesting buildings throw open their doors. *Late May.*

JUNE

Luminato Festival A 19-day arts festival with music, dance, film, literature, theater and visual arts. Various venues. *Jun.*
North by Northeast (NXNE) Toronto rocks for 10 days with 1,000 bands in more than 45 venues, plus comedians, music movies, speakers and eSports competitions. *Mid-Jun.*
Pride Toronto Festival An arts and culture festival, including a huge Pride Parade, that fills more than three weeks of events. *Mid-Jun.*
TD Toronto Jazz Festival Fun along Toronto's waterfront from Spadina to Sherbourne. *Jun.*

JULY

Canada Day Open-air concerts, fireworks and other events. *Jul 1.*
Redpath Waterfront Festival Four (nonconsecutive) nights of spectacular fireworks set to music. Ontario Place. *Late Jun/early Jul.*
Toronto Fringe Festival An eclectic mix of theatrical events. *Early Jul.*
Toronto's Festival of Beer More than 120

brews, including Ontario craft beers. *Late Jul.*
Salsa in Toronto Festival Three weeks of Latino
celebrations, including a two-day street party.
Throughout Jul.
Honda Indy Toronto A week of motor racing,
entertainment and activities. *Mid-Jul.*
Toronto Caribbean Carnival Calypso,
reggae, steel bands and soca. Exhibition Place
and other venues. *Jul/mid-Aug.*

AUGUST
*Canadian National Exhibition and International
Air Show* Three-week fair, including an air
show. Exhibition Place. *Mid-Aug/early Sep.*

SEPTEMBER
Canada's Walk of Fame Festival Music, film,
dance and comedy. Massey Hall and other
venues. *Mid-Sep.*
The Word on the Street Festival National literary festival featuring readings, storytelling and
other events in various venues. *Late Sep.*
Toronto Oktoberfest Get out your lederhosen
to enjoy Bavarian fare, bands and beer. Ontario
Place parking lot. *Late Sep/early Oct.*

OCTOBER
Art Toronto One of the finest art events in
Canada. *Late Oct.*

NOVEMBER
Santa Claus Parade A Toronto tradition since
1905, the parade has colorful floats, marching
bands, and thousands of costumed participants.
Along Bloor Street West. *Mid-Nov.*
Cavalcade of Lights The lighting of Toronto's
Christmas tree at Nathan Phillips Square. Music,
fireworks and ice skating. *Late Nov.*

DECEMBER
Tafelmusik's Sing-Along Messiah Fun
Christmas event at Massey Hall. *Few days
before Dec 24.*
CityTV New Year's Eve Nathan Phillips Square is
packed with revelers. *Dec 31.*

CULTURAL FEASTS

In this multicultural city, a
number of excellent festivals relate to the various
"old countries" and they
provide a great way to
learn about the cultures
that are being kept alive—
not to mention the wonderful food. They include the
colorful Chinese New Year
in Chinatown (Jan/Feb);
Taste of Little Italy, based
on College Street (Bathurst
to Shaw), in mid-June;
Taste of the Danforth,
celebrating Greektown
and its food and culture
in mid-August; the Festival
of South Asia, on Gerrard
Street East (Coxwell to
Greenwood) in mid-August
and the same neighbor-
hood's Diwali celebration
in mid-November; Bloor
West Village Ukrainian
Festival and the Hispanic
Fiesta on Mel Lastman
Square, Yonge Street, both
from late August to early
September; Roncesvalles
Polish Festival, in the village
in west Toronto, in mid-
September.

Timeline

REBELLION

The first mayor of Toronto, William Lyon Mackenzie, shared immigrant aspirations for political reform and campaigned vehemently against the narrow-minded, exclusive power of the Family Compact—a group of ardent British loyalists who controlled the city's economy and politics. By 1837 he was advocating open rebellion, and on December 5 around 700 rebels assembled at Montgomery's Tavern. Led by Mackenzie, they marched on the city. The sheriff called out the militia, who scattered the rebels at Carlton Street. Mackenzie fled to the United States. Two other ringleaders were hanged.

Left to right: A polished stone Inuit carving in the Inuit Gallery; an ornate Inuit mask in the Bay of Spirits Gallery; an ancient Inuit painting, The Shaman's Wife, *in the Kleinburg Museum*

1720 France sets up a trading post at the Humber River.

1750 Fort Rouillé (Fort Toronto) is built.

1763 The Treaty of Paris secures Canada for Britain.

1787 The British purchase land from the Mississauga tribe on which Toronto will be sited.

1793 John Graves Simcoe, Governor of Upper Canada, arrives and names the settlement York.

1813 Americans invade, destroy Fort York and burn Parliament Buildings.

1834 The city is named Toronto ("meeting place"). William Lyon Mackenzie becomes the first mayor.

1837 Former mayor, Mackenzie, leads rebellion against the Family Compact (▷ panel).

1844 George Brown founds The Globe.

1858 The Toronto Islands are created from a peninsula smashed by a violent storm.

1867 Canadian Confederation: Toronto becomes capital of Ontario province.

1884 The streets are lit by electricity.

1914–18 70,000 Torontonians enlist and 13,000 are killed in World War I.

1920 The Group of Seven hold their first art exhibition.

1923 The Chinese Exclusion Act restricts Chinese immigration.

1933 The Depression leads to 30 percent unemployment.

1950 Sunday sports are permitted.

1953 Metro plans under way.

1995 The Conservative Government is elected and focuses on budget cuts.

1996 *Fortune* magazine names Toronto "Best City for Work and Family outside the US."

1998 Toronto's six municipalities merge.

2002/3 Toronto Transit's new Sheppard Line connects North York to downtown.

2007 A redevelopment of Toronto Pearson International Airport is completed.

2010 Toronto hosts the G-20 summit.

2015 Toronto hosts PanAm Games.

2017 Toronto hosts Invictus Games.

BUILDING TORONTO

1844 First City Hall
1845 King's College
1851 St. Lawrence Hall
1852 The Toronto Stock Exchange
1869 Eaton's
1886 The Provincial Parliament buildings
1907 The Royal Alexander
1912 The Royal Ontario Museum
1931 Maple Leaf Gardens arena
1965 New City Hall
1971 Ontario Place
1972 Harbourfront development
1975 CN Tower
1989 SkyDome stadium
1993 CBC Building
2006 Four Seasons Centre for the Performing Arts
2007 Michael Lee-Chin Crystal at ROM
2008 Art Gallery of Ontario redevelopment
2017 Downtown waterfront development continues

Left to right: An interpreter in 19th-century British military uniform in the grounds of Fort York; models of Stone Age hunters in the Royal Ontario Museum

Index

Toronto 25 Best

WRITTEN BY Marilyn Wood
ADDITIONAL WRITING BY Penny Phenix
UPDATED BY Penny Phenix
SERIES EDITOR Clare Ashton
COVER DESIGN Chie Ushio, Yuko Inagaki
DESIGN WORK Tom Whitlock and Liz Baldin
IMAGE RETOUCHING AND REPRO Ian Little

Published in the United Kingdom by AA Publishing

ISBN 978-1-64097-098-4

EIGHTH EDITION

Color separation by AA Digital Department
Printed and bound by Leo Paper Products, China

10 9 8 7 6 5 4 3 2 1

A05593
Maps in this title produced from mapping data supplied by Global Mapping, Brackley, UK © Global Mapping
Transport map © Communicarta Ltd, UK

The Automobile Association would like to thank the following photographers, companies and picture libraries for their assistance in the preparation of this book.

2-18 AA/N Sumner; 4c AA/N Sumner; 5c ROM/Sam Javanrouh; 6cl AA/J Davison; 6c AA/N Sumner; 6cr Imagestate; 6bl AA/N Sumner; 6bc Canoe, Oliver Bonacini Restauarants; 6br AA DigitalVision; 7c Tourism Toronto; 7cr AA/J Davison; 7bl AA/N Sumner; 7bc AA/A Mockford & N Bonetti; 7br AA/N Sumner; 10/11t Tourism Toronto; 10c AA/C Sawyer; 10/11c AA/N Sumner; 10/11b © Prisma Bildagentur AG / Alamy Stock Photo; 11c © Arseny Barkovskiy /Alamy Stock Photo; 13ct AA/N Sumner; 13c © Robert Harding World Imagery /Alamy Stock Photo; 13b AA/N Sumner; 14ct AA/N Sumner; 14cb AA/P Enticknap; 14c Bymark/McEwan Group; 14b AA/N Sumner; 16ct AA/J Davison; 16/17ct Distillery District ; 16/17cb Distillery District; 16br The Legislative Assembly of Ontario; 17ct Tourism Toronto, Toronto Island Cyclists; 17b AA/N Sumner; 18ct Distillery District; 18c AA DigitalVision; 18br AA Photodisc; 19t AA/N Sumner; 19ct AA/J Davison; 19c AA/N Sumner; 19cb AA/J Davison; 19b AA/N Sumner; 20/21 Torontonian/Alamy Stock Photo; 24 Reimar 4/Alamy Stock Photo; 25t AA/N Sumner; 25bl David Giral /Alamy Stock Photo; 25br Torontonian/Alamy Stock Photo; 26l AA/N Sumner; 26tr CN Tower; 27cl AA/N Sumner; 27cr AA/N Sumner; 28 City of Toronto; 29t City of Toronto; 29cl City of Toronto; 29cr AA/J Davison; 30l AA/N Sumner; 30c AA/N Sumner; 30r AA/N Sumner; 31l Ripley's Aquarium of Canada; 31r Ripley's Aquarium of Canada; 32l Eden Breitz /Alamy Stock Photo; 34 AA/N Sumner; 35-36 AA/N Sumner; 37-38 AA/N Sumner; 39-40 AA/C Sawyer; 41 City of Toronto; 44 AA/N Sumner; 44/45t AA/N Sumner; 44/45c AA/N Sumner; 45cl AA/N Sumner; 45cr Kyle90~commonswiki/File:Toronto City Hall Lobby.jpg; 46 Design Exchange; 47t Design Exchange; 47cl Design Exchange; 47cr Design Exchange; 48 Distillery District; 49tl Distillery District/Thane Lucas-lucasdigitalart.com; 49tr Distillery District/Thane Lucas-lucasdigitalart.com; 49cl Distillery District/Thane Lucas-lucasdigitalart.com; 49cr Distillery District; 50l AA/J Davison; 50r AA/J Davison; 51l City of Toronto St. Lawrence Hall; 51r City of Toronto St. Lawrence Market; 52t-53t AA/N Sumner; 52 Torontonian/ Alamy Stock Photo; 53t Marc Bruxelle/Alamy Stock Photo; 53c AGF Srl/Alamy Stock Photo; 54b Courtesy of Tourism Toronto; 55bl Textile Museum; 55br Textile Museum; 56 City of Toronto St. Lawrence Market; 57 AA/N Sumner; 58 AA/N Sumner; 59 AA/C Sawyer; 60 AA/C Sawyer; 61 Bert Hoferichter/Alamy Stock Photo; 63cr BiR Fotos/ Stockimo/Alamy Stock Photo; 64l AA/N Sumner; 64/65 AA/N Sumner; 65t Eyepix/ Alamy Stock Photo; 65c AA/N Sumner; 66l Tourism Toronto, Toronto Island; 66/7t Ana Clara Tito/Alamy Stock Photo; 66/67c AA/J Davison; 66cr Tourism Toronto, Toronto Island; 66c AA/N Sumner; 68bl Tourism Toronto; 68br Tourism Toronto; 69 AA/N Sumner; 70 Tourism Toronto; 71 AA/N Sumner; 72 AA/N Sumner; 73 BiR Fotos/Stockimo/Alamy Stock Photo; 74 AA/C Sawyer; 75 Casa Loma Conservatory; 78-79t Bata Shoe Museum; 78-79b AA/J Davison; 78l AA/N Sumner; 79t Bata Shoe Museum; 79c AA/J Davison; 79r AA/J Davison; 80l AA/J Davison; 80r Casa Loma; 81l Gardiner Museum; 81r Gardiner Museum; 82/3 ROM/Sam Javanrouh; 83t ROM; 83c ROM; 83cr ROM; 84-86t AA/N Sumner; 84l © Design Pics Inc./Alamy Stock Photo; 84r AA/J Beazley; 85 AA/J Davison; 87 AA/N Sumner; 88 AA/N Sumner; 89 AA DigitalVision; 90 AA/C Sawyer; 91 Canada's Wonderland; 94l AA/N Sumner; 94r AA/N Sumner; 95l Canada's Wonderland; 95r Canada's Wonderland; 96l City of Toronto; 96r City of Toronto; 97l McMichael Canadian Art Collection; 97r Bill Brooks/Alamy Stock Photo; 98l Museum of Contemporary Art; 99 Arash Moallemi; 100/101t Ontario Science Centre; 100l Ontario Science Centre; 100/1b Ontario Science Centre; 101cr Ontario Science Centre; 102l AA/N Sumner; 102br AA/N Sumner; 103t AA/N Sumner; 103bl African Lion Safari; 103br AA/N Sumner; 104t AA/N Sumner; 104bl Tourism Toronto; 105-106 AA/N Sumner; 107 © National Geographic Image Collection/Alamy Stock Photo; 108t-112t AA/C Sawyer; 108ct AA Photodisc; 108c AA Photodisc; 108cb AA Photodisc; 108b AA/S McBride; 113 AA/N Sumner; 114-125 AA/N Sumner; 124bl AA/J Davison; 124bc AA/J Davison; 124br AA/J Francois Pin; 125bl AA/J Davison; 125br AA/J Davison

Every effort has been made to trace the copyright holders, and we apologize in advance for any accidental errors. We would be happy to apply the corrections in the following edition of this publication.

Titles in the Series